D1474694

FRONTISPIECE: *top left : Cream Layer Cake (80) ; top right : Doughnuts (88) —
note special pan; bottom left: Whipped Cream Cones (105);
bottom right : Damson Tart (106)*

Danish Home Baking

TRADITIONAL DANISH RECIPES

COMPILED BY

Kaj Viktor og Kirsten Hansen

AND EDITED BY

Karen Berg

Dover Publications, Inc.
New York

This Dover edition, first published in 1972, is an unabridged republication of the second (1960) edition of the work originally published in 1957 by Andr. Fred. Høst & Søn, Copenhagen.

The color photographs on the book covers and the black and white photographs within in the book are by Niels Elswing.

The book is reprinted by special arrangement with Høst & Søns Forlag, Copenhagen.

International Standard Book Number: 0-486-22863-0
Library of Congress Catalog Card Number: 72-78002

Manufactured in the United States of America
Dover Publications, Inc.
180 Varick Street
New York, N. Y. 10014

CONTENTS

Salt of hartshorn, an ingredient called for in several of the recipes, is another name for ammonium chloride or ammonium carbonate. It can be procured through a pharmacy.

FOREWORD

We Danes are rather proud of the democratic way we think we run our country, proud of our social welfare set-up and all that. But we have to admit that in the course of history there have been some autocratic monarchs who have also managed to think up some bright ideas for making life more cheerful. Our whole-hearted approval, for instance, goes to Marie Antoinette for propounding the famous doctrine: "Give them cake!"

We love cake in any shape or form; though of course, being patriotic, we have a sneaking preference for our own shapes and forms. We like large cakes and small cakes; loaf cakes and layer cakes; 'heavenly mouthfuls' and monumental whipped cream cakes; cookies and pastries, custard pies and damson tarts. In fact we like practically anything that is sweet and has been baked in an oven.

We like pastries for breakfast—our own particular brand, which we choose to call, for some obscure reason, "Viennese Bread". We don't say no to them in the middle of the morning if a friend suggests going and having a couple together with a cup of coffee. And we like them again (with another cup of coffee) to top off a sandwich lunch.

In the afternoons we like coffee-parties instead of tea-parties. We like to start them at about 3 o'clock instead of 4 or 5 o'clock, the idea being to give our guests (and ourselves) plenty of time to try at least one of each different kind of cake or cookie before dinner comes round.

We have our dinners in the evening at about 6 or 6.30. We have to admit that we are not madly keen on the boiled puddings of our friends the British across the North Sea. Frankly, we prefer cake—but we call it "dessert". The difference is perhaps not always so very apparent; but whereas the cold, analytical eye will observe that many of our cakes tend to feature some form of pastry garnished with whipped cream, raspberry jam, vanilla custard and/or stewed fruit, many of our favorite desserts merely feature whipped cream, raspberry jam, vanilla custard and/or stewed fruit. In other words we wisely omit, now and again, the pastry, remembering that it can be a little fattening.

Around 8 or 9 o'clock in the evening our national weakness is to indulge in another little cup of coffee (or tea) with another little piece of cake (or a few cookies).

And so to bed.

Thus a day in the life of a Dane is inclined to be a cakeful day. But try your hand at some of the recipes in this book and maybe you will see why!

COOKIES & CHRISTMAS COOKIES

COOKIES

Danes are frequently accused of having rather lax conceptions of "etiquette". When it comes to the point it generally seems to be we ourselves who do most of the accusing. In fact we often take mischievous delight (we call it mischievous) in accepting such accusations with glee and pretending to be far more easy-going and carefree than we really are.

One respect however, in which we continually find ourselves suffering from our yearning for the informal, is in the matter of "unexpected visitors". We love being "unexpected visitors". We love dropping in on our friends without previous warning and like to time our visits to coincide as closely as possible with a moment when we can reasonably expect them to be just about to sit down to a cup of coffee. We never protest more than once or twice if asked to remove our overcoats and come in; and although we insist, almost convincingly, that we had a cup of coffee ourselves just before we left home, we can usually be persuaded after a jolly bout of "Honestly, I couldn't!" and "But really, you must just

try a *little* piece!", to sit down after all and tuck in
with a will.

The result of this informal national habit is that
the average Danish housewife lives under the con-
stant shadow of "what to offer the unexpected
visitor". And the only sound remedy to the problem,
as most Danish housewives found out years and
years ago, is to take time off every now and again to
bake a few pounds of cookies, put them away in an
air-tight tin and face the morrow with a mind at
ease, prepared to meet any invasion.

Here follow a number of recipes for such cookies.
They are all favorites in Denmark and no "unexpected visitor" will fail to compliment his or her
hostess on their delectability—and ask her discreetly
how many eggs she used.

1. VANILLA WREATHS I
Vanillekranse

(makes approx. 150)

3 ½ cups flour
2 ¼ cups sugar
1 ½ cups butter
2 eggs
½ cup *finely* chopped almonds
vanilla

Of all Danish cookies, these are probably the most
widely popular. The first recipe, on account of the
extra butter and the almonds, is more expensive than
the second. Danish children seem to like the raw
batter just as much as the finished article, so be on the
watch-out for small fingers poking over the edge of
your mixing-bowl. A pastry tube produces more

OPPOSITE: *top : two varieties of Meringue (12); in basket, from top center,
clockwise: Vanilla Wreaths (1), Coconut Macaroons (8), Oatmeal
Macaroons (10), Jutlanders (6), Flatties (4), Strasbourgers (7), Jewish
Cakes (5).*

artistic results in both cases, but many Danish housewives work wonders with a meat-grinder fitted with
a special mouthpiece.

Mix sugar and eggs. Stir in butter, almonds,
vanilla and finally the flour. Grease cookie sheet well
with butter. Place batter in pastry tube and squirt out
on to sheet in small rings. Bake in slow oven until
golden brown.

2. VANILLA WREATHS II
Vanillekranse

(makes approx. 150)
3 ½ cups flour
1 ⅓ cups butter

½ cup sugar
1 cup powdered sugar
1 whole egg
1 yolk of egg
pinch of salt of hartshorn
vanilla

Mix all the ingredients together into a dough and set
aside to cool for about 30 mins. Squirt out on the
table in long strips using a pastry tube. Cut into
lengths of about 3 ins. and form into rings. Grease
cookie sheet well with butter. Bake in slow oven
until golden brown.

3. SUGARED PRETZELS
Kringler

(makes approx. 130)

3 ½ cups flour
1 cup butter
1 egg
1 teaspoon baking powder
½ cup cream

The pretzel is the trade sign of the Danish baker. The
shape is used not only for salted crackers but also for
cakes, pastries and, as in the following recipe,
cookies. It doesn't matter whether your knot looks

more like a "grannie" than a reef-knot—they taste just as good either way!

Work all the ingredients together into a dough and set aside to cool off for approx. 30 mins. Cut into small pieces and roll into thin rolls between the palms. Form into pretzel shapes and dip top sides in crystalized sugar. Grease cookie sheet well with butter. Bake golden brown in slow oven.

4. FLATTIES
Pleskner

(makes approx. 70)

3 eggs
⅔ cup sugar
1 ½ cups flour
a few grains of salt of hartshorn

These take no time at all and are very easy to make —even for children.

Beat eggs and sugar to a stiff batter. Fold in flour and salt of hartshorn carefully. Place in pastry tube and squirt out in small round shapes on to a greased cookie sheet. Bake golden brown in slow oven.

5. JEWISH CAKES
Jødekager

(makes approx. 180)
2 ½ cups flour
1 ¼ cups butter

½ cup cream
1 ⅓ cup sugar
1 whole egg
1 yolk of egg
pinch of salt of hartshorn
almond sugar, or cinnamon sugar

Mix butter, sugar and eggs well, then stir in flour, cream and salt of hartshorn. Set aside to cool. Roll out thin and cut into cookie shapes with a wineglass.

Brush with egg white and sprinkle with either almond sugar or cinnamon sugar. Bake golden brown in slow oven.

6. JUTLANDERS
Jydske Specier

(makes approx. 64)

1 ½ cups flour
⅔ cup butter
1 ¼ tablespoons powdered sugar
1 teaspoon vanilla sugar

"Specie" is an old-fashioned Danish word for a "rigsdaler", or "dollar" of the times. Children soon find out that these cookies roll across the floor very easily on their edges, so keep the cookie jar well out of reach!

Knead all the ingredients into a dough and form into two rolls approx. 1½ ins. in diameter. Set aside to cool until stiff and then slice each roll into approx. 32 pieces with a sharp knife. Bake in slow oven until golden brown.

7. STRASBOURGERS
Strassburger

(makes approx. 100)

⅔ cup butter
1 ¼ cups powdered sugar
2 cups flour
1 teaspoon vanilla sugar
1 egg

The name does not sound very Danish, but these cookies have had their place in Danish cookie-jars for generations. Somebody probably 'lifted' the recipe from Strasbourg because they thought it was worth 'lifting'.

Cream butter and powdered sugar until white. Add flour and vanilla sugar. Mix well. Grease cookie sheet. Place in pastry tube with star-shaped tip and press out on to cookie sheet in small, zig-zag-shaped cakes. Bake golden brown in slow oven.

8. COCONUT MACAROONS
Kokusmakroner

(makes approx. 35)

2 cups coconut flour
½ cup sugar
1 cup powdered sugar
3 whites of egg
pinch of salt of hartshorn
vanilla

A fairly internationally-known cookie this, but who could resist including the recipe?

Mix coconut flour, sugar and powdered sugar in a pot. Add whites of egg. Toast until fairly warm, then add salt of hartshorn and vanilla. Remove from heat and drop batter by tablespoons on to a greased and floured cookie sheet in pointed clumps. Bake pale golden brown.

9. CURRANT COOKIES
Korendekager

(makes approx. 150)
1 cup butter
1 cup sugar

1⅔ cups flour
2 cups corn starch
3 eggs
grated rind and juice of ½ a
    lemon
pinch of salt of hartshorn
currants

Cream butter and sugar until white. Stir in eggs one at a time. Finally add flour, corn starch, salt of hartshorn, grated lemon rind and juice. Stir well. Drop off on cookie sheet with a teaspoon. *Before* baking place 4–5 currants on the top of each cookie. Bake until pale golden in slow oven.

10. OATMEAL MACAROONS
Havremakroner

(makes approx. 150)

½ cup butter
1 ½ cups oatmeal
1 ½ cups sugar
⅔ cup flour
2 ½ teaspoons baking powder
3 eggs
⅔ cup *finely* chopped almonds

Despite the fact that almonds are very expensive in Denmark, we just can't resist putting them in wherever we can—they certainly help put these oatmeal macaroons in a class by themselves!

Mix sugar and oatmeal in a bowl. Melt butter, allow to cool off and then pour over the oatmeal-sugar mixture. Stir well, sift in flour and baking powder and finally add the eggs and chopped almonds. Grease cookie sheet with butter. Drop off on to cookie sheet with a *small* teaspoon and leave plenty of space between each cookie as they spread out a lot. Bake golden brown in slow oven.

11. RUSKS
Kammerjunkere

(makes approx. 250)

1 oz. yeast
2 tablespoons sugar
2 eggs
½ cup butter
3 cups flour
1 teaspoon salt
½ cup milk

In Denmark we often serve these rusks with various kinds of hot fruit soups. Unfortunately, foreigners never seem to be able to work up much enthusiasm for our fruit soups (we admit it takes generations of practice) but this does not prevent the rusks themselves from being excellent just as they are, served with coffee or tea.

Warm milk slightly. Add eggs, yeast, sugar, salt and butter, a little of each at a time, and stir the lot well. Stir in flour until you get a good stiff dough. Wrap in a cloth sprinkled with a little flour. Set aside to rise in a warm place for about 30 mins. After the first 15 mins. have passed, press the air out of the dough so that it tightens up and leave it to "rest" for the last 15 mins. Form into long rolls about the thickness of your thumb. Cut each roll into small pieces and shape them into tiny buns. Let rise again for about 15 mins. Bake golden brown in hot oven. When the buns are cold, cut them in two with a sharp knife, put them back in a slow oven close together on the cookie sheet and let them dry out until they are crisp and golden brown. Keep in an air-tight tin.

12. MERINGUES
Marengs

(makes approx. 60)
3 large whites of egg
¾ cup sugar
1 teaspoon vinegar

Meringues in Denmark are also known as 'kisses', maybe because they are just as sweet, or maybe because one always wants just one more.

Mix egg whites and sugar in the top of a double boiler. Heat until sugar melts, *stirring continuously*.

Remove and whip up into a stiff froth while still warm. Cover cookie sheet with a piece of thin paper and squirt batter out in small clumps. Bake in very slow oven for about 30 mins. As a variation you can color the ready-whipped batter with fruit juice and sprinkle with colored shot. Make these meringues smaller (see illustration). Serve with coffee, tea, or with ice-cream as a dessert.

13. CHOCOLATE MERINGUES
Chokolademarengs

(makes approx. 60)
1 large egg white
2 cups powdered sugar
1 oz. cocoa (just under)
1 oz. chopped nuts

Mix powdered sugar with the egg white. Add cocoa and chopped nuts, also a very little water if necessary. The batter should be soft but firm. Sift a little powdered sugar out on the table and roll out batter approx. ½ in. thick. Cut into small round cookies or crescents. Place on floured cookie sheet and bake in slow oven.

CHRISTMAS COOKIES

There are three kinds of cookies traditional in all Danish homes at Christmastime: "Brown Cakes", "Peppernuts" and a kind of cruller known as "Smalls". "Brown Cakes" and "Peppernuts" are richly spiced. No two Danish housewives use exactly the same spices in their batter, nor exactly the same quantities. Most of them scorn the recipes given in Danish cook-books, insisting that the only person who really knew how to bake "Brown Cakes" (or was it "Peppernuts"?) was Mother, Grandma, or Aunt Birgitte.

14. "PEPPERNUTS"
Pebernødder

(makes approx. 400)
1 cup sirup
½ cup sugar

¼ cup butter
3 ½ cups flour
1 teaspoon crushed cloves
1 teaspoon cinnamon
grated rind of 1 lemon
½ oz. potash
pinch of salt of hartshorn

This sounds like an awful lot of Peppernuts. But Christmas lasts quite a long time and no Danish family has ever found they had enough of them.

Boil sirup, butter and sugar together in a pot. When cool, sift in the rest of the ingredients. The dough must be allowed to stand for 48 hours, preferably in a warm place. Knead dough again and roll out to ½ in. thickness. Cut into small pieces and form into balls. Place on greased cookie sheet and bake in moderate oven.

15. "SMALLS"
Klejner

(makes approx. 150)
4 cups flour

1 cup butter
¼ cup cream
½ cup sugar
½ teaspoon salt of hartshorn
3 eggs
vanilla

An old Danish Christmas custom demands that no visitor to your house during Christmas may be allowed to leave without having tasted your Christmas cookies—otherwise you run the risk of the visitor's 'carrying the Christmas spirit away'. So you might as well make a double portion of these while you are at it.

Mix all the ingredients together into a dough and set aside to cool for about half an hour. Roll out thin and cut into long strips about $1\frac{1}{4}$ ins. wide. Cut the strips across diagonally into smaller strips about $3\frac{1}{2}$ ins. in length. In the middle of each of these smaller pieces make a slash with the point of a knife. Pull one end of the piece through the slash to form a half-knot. Drop into boiling fat and cook until golden brown, turning now and again with a fork. Lift out with a perforated spoon and place in a strainer to allow the fat to drip off.

16. "BROWN CAKES"
Brune Kager

(makes approx. 300)
$1\frac{2}{3}$ cups sirup
1 cup brown sugar
$\frac{1}{4}$ cup butter

4 cups flour
$\frac{1}{2}$ oz. potash
$\frac{1}{2}$ teaspoon salt of hartshorn
$\frac{1}{4}$ oz. crushed cinnamon
$\frac{1}{4}$ oz. ginger
$\frac{1}{4}$ oz. cardamom
grated rind of 1 lemon
almonds

Melt the butter in a pot. Add sirup and brown sugar and heat. Stir in the spices, then the potash and the salt of hartshorn (previously dissolved in a little water). When cool, sift in flour and let the batter stand 24 hours. Roll out very thin. Cut into round shapes with a wineglass, or diamonds, or squares, or, if you are feeling ambitious and want to enter into the Christmas spirit, form little men, women, hearts, flags etc. Brush with water. Stick a whole almond on the top of each cookie, or else a few chopped pieces. Bake in a slow oven.

Section 2

SMALL CAKES & PARTY CAKES

These are generally served and eaten at 3 o'clock coffee parties in Denmark, especially on Sunday afternoons. Some are simple enough, but others require fairly nimble fingers and a well-organized kitchen with all the necessary ingredients and implements at hand. There is nothing quite so exasperating as embarking on, for instance, *Rum tops* (35) and halfway through the operation discovering that you have forgotten to lay in a stock of cocktail cherries.

It would be misleading to suggest that all Danish housewives are equally skilful at conjuring up all the little cakes in this section. Many newly-weds (and a few older-weds) in Copenhagen and the big towns would probably confess, if you asked them, that they prefer to send some member of the family round to the nearest baker's or confectioner's to buy the professional article. "Some member of the family", in Denmark, nearly always means Father—indeed, the quiet streets of Copenhagen on a Sunday afternoon from roughly 2 o'clock onwards are a somewhat strange sight to the uninitiated; there always seems to be a preponderance of lone, not very happy-looking males, wandering along clutching white paper packets, cunningly wrapped with yards of stiff paper to prevent the beauty of their contents from being spoiled by ham-handed Daddy on his way home.

However, if you enjoy having a bit of fun in your kitchen, have a go at baking them yourself for a change. The odds are they will be better, probably fresher, and quite definitely cheaper.

17. MEDALS
Medaljer

(makes approx. 75)
3 ½ cups flour
1 ½ cups powdered sugar
1 cup butter
4 yolks of egg

These medals are not merely awarded for bravery—they are given to anybody who deserves an extra special treat! Though 'professional' cakes they are really very easy to make—and many other variations can be made from the same dough (see Nos. 18, 20, 21, 23 and 42).

Work flour and butter together with the fingers, add powdered sugar and egg yolks and mix all ingredients well. Roll out dough thin and cut into round cookie shapes with a medium-sized wineglass. Place on a greased cookie sheet and bake in a moderate oven until pale golden. Can be kept in an airtight tin until required.

Take twice as many cookie-shapes as the number of cakes you wish to make. Glaze half of them with

sugar icing (42) and spread vanilla custard (41) on the
root. Sandwich the glazed cookies (glazed side up) on
top of these, spread with custard and decorate with a
small square of hard red jelly.

18. CUSTARD PIES (makes approx. 75)

I inser

It cannot be denied that, as a nation, our idea of a
cake worthy of the name is one that includes a
generous tot of whipped cream. But now and again
even we hanker after what we call a "dry cake" and
in such instances we feel there is little to beat these
custard pies.

Make same dough as for 17. Roll out thin. Grease
small cake forms (preferably smooth-sided). Cut
dough to appropriately sized shapes and place in
forms. Fill with vanilla custard (41) and cover with
a "lid" of same dough. Press edges together lightly
and bake for about 20 mins. in a good fast oven.

19. CREAM PUFFS

Vandbakkelser

(makes approx. 30)

½ cup margarine
1 ½ cups flour
6 eggs
pinch of salt of hartshorn
powdered sugar *or* chocolate
    icing (42)
1 cup water

We call them "water puffs", which is an understate-
ment. The English name "cream puffs" does them
far more justice and to be quite honest, we wish we
had thought of it first.

22. BUTTERCREAM
Smørcreme

1 cup butter
1 cup shortening
2 cups powdered sugar
5 eggs
vanilla

Cream butter and shortening until smooth. Stir in the sifted sugar until the mass is white. Add eggs one at a time and stir again well. Finally stir in vanilla.

23. APPLE SQUARES
Æblesnitter

(makes approx. 50)

dough as for 17
apple jam
bread crumbs
crystalized sugar
almonds

When it comes to using fruit to brighten a cake, you will never go far wrong with the common apple. Incidentally, we think these are better with coffee than with tea.

Roll out half of the dough (not too thin) and place on oven sheet (should be roughly same size). Sprinkle thinly with bread crumbs and then spread a thin layer of apple jam on top. Roll out the other half of the dough to same size and thickness and place on top of the apple. Brush with egg and sprinkle with crystalized sugar and finely chopped almonds. Bake golden brown in fairly hot oven. When cold cut into conveniently sized squares or rectangles.

CAKES MADE WITH PUFF PASTE

Puff paste consists of flour, butter and water and can be used for a great number of cakes. On the following pages, recipes are given for 8 variations.

24. PUFF PASTE
Butterdejg

3 ½ cups flour
2 cups butter
1 cup *cold* water
1 tablespoon vinegar

Sift flour and work into ¹/₅ of the butter. Add vinegar and water. Knead well into a smooth dough that slides easily on the table and in the hands. Set aside to cool for a few moments. Sprinkle table with a little flour and place dough on it. Place the rest of the butter on the top of the dough and pack the dough up round the butter. Now roll out in a square about ½ in. thick. Fold the two ends inwards so that they meet in the middle. Fold once again so that the dough is now four layers thick. Roll out again in a slightly elongated square. Fold again as before, i.e. first the two ends so that they meet in the middle, then once again. The dough has now been rolled and folded twice, but *must be rolled and folded twice more in exactly the same way*. After each of the first two rollings it must be set aside to cool for about 10 mins. When rolled out for the last time, set aside to cool and stiffen, whereupon it is ready for use.

25. NAPOLEON CAKES
Napoleonskager

(makes approx. 40)
puff paste (24)
vanilla custard (41)
sugar icing (42)
raspberry jam

Nobody in Denmark is quite sure how these cakes got the name "Napoleon", though it is presumed that some Danish baker's apprentice picked up the

OPPOSITE: *on white plate, from top: Apple Purses (27), Fans (29), Crispies (31); top left: Rum Tops and other variations (33 to 38); bottom right: Napoleon Cakes (25), Medals (17), Cream Puffs (19), Raspberry Tarts (20); bottom left: Hans Andersen Cakes (42).*

recipe during the course of his wanderings and studies in France, brought it home and decided to dub the cakes something that sounded both French and exciting. The French themselves call them '*mille feuilles*' (thousand leaves) which, though equally exciting, is maybe a slight exaggeration.

Roll out a piece of puff paste thinly to roughly the size of your oven sheet, place thereon and let it stand for about 15 mins. Cut down lengthways into four strips and *prick well with a fork*. Bake in fairly slow oven until light and crisp. When cold, glaze two of the strips with sugar icing (44). On the two remaining strips spread first a layer of raspberry jam and on top of this a layer of vanilla custard (43). Place the glazed strips (glazed side upwards) on the top of the custard. Cut into conveniently sized cakes with a sharp knife. These cakes should be eaten roughly within the hour after being "built" as otherwise they tend to become soggy.

26. DAMSON TARTS
Svedsketærte

(makes approx. 40)
puff paste (24)
damson jam
powdered sugar
whipped cream

Prepare puff paste as for 24. On two of the strips spread a thick layer of damson jam and cover up with the two remaining strips. Sprinkle with a thin layer of powdered sugar. Cut into convenient lengths with a sharp knife and decorate with a rosette of whipped cream. As with *Napoleon Cakes* (25), should be served within the hour.

27. APPLE PURSES
Æbletasker

(makes approx. 30)
puff paste (24)
apple jam
crystalized sugar
almonds
1 egg for brushing

Roll out a piece of puff paste to a thickness of about $^3/_8$ in. and cut into round shapes with a large tumbler. Place a heaped tablespoonful of jam in the middle of each, fold over like an omelet and press edges well together. Brush top sides with egg. Dip in a mixture of chopped almonds and crystalized sugar. Bake golden brown and crisp in moderate oven (not too hot).

28. PRINCESS SUGAR PRETZELS
Prinsessekringler

(makes approx. 60)
puff paste (24)
crystalized sugar
almonds
1 egg for brushing

Another member of the Danish pretzel family—and indeed a princess of the realm!

Roll out a piece of puff paste to an oblong shape about $^3/_8$ in. thick and about 5 ins. wide. Brush with egg and sprinkle with chopped almonds and crystalized sugar. Cut (diagonally across) into strips about ³/₈ in. wide and twist these into pretzel shapes. Set aside to cool for 15 mins. before baking them pale golden and crisp in a moderate oven. Keep in an air-tight tin, preferably in a warm place.

29. FANS
Vifter

(makes approx. 60)
puff paste (24)
sugar

The only difference between this recipe and the one that follows is that these really do look quite like fans, whereas the ones we choose to call "Donkeys' Ears" don't look like donkeys' ears at all. But after all, what's in a name?

Roll out a piece of puff paste very thin and about 12 ins. wide, length as desired. Sprinkle with a thin layer of sugar and roll up into a tight roll. Place in refrigerator until stiff. Cut into slices about ¼ in. thick and place on baking sheet. Make a single cut in each from the center to the edge so that during baking they will spread out in the shape of a fan. Bake golden and crisp in a fast oven.

30. DONKEYS' EARS
Æselører

(makes approx. 50)
puff paste (24)
sugar

Roll out puff paste as for 29. Sprinkle with sugar and roll both ends tightly in towards the middle. Set aside to cool and then cut into slices about ¼ in. thick. Bake pale golden and crisp in fast oven.

31. CRISPIES

Snitter

(makes approx. 40)
puff paste (24)
1 yolk of egg for brushing

Please note these are *not* served at coffee-parties, but are best with fish and chicken dishes. We include the recipe in this section because while on the subject of puff paste it would be a pity to leave it out.

Roll out a piece of puff paste to a thickness of about $^3/_8$ in. Cut into strips 2 ins. wide. Cut each strip (diagonally) into smaller pieces each again about 2 ins. wide. Place on baking sheet and brush with egg yolk. It is important to brush them only on the top sides so that none of the egg flows over the edges. Set aside to cool for 20 mins. before putting them in to bake until pale golden in a fast oven.

32. PATTY SHELLS

Tarteletter

(makes approx. 40)
puff paste (24)

Recipe included here for same reasons as in 31. Served with a filling of peas, chopped ham, asparagus, chicken, meat leftovers etc.

Roll out a piece of puff paste to a thickness of about ¼ in. Cut out and place in small, deep cake forms. Press well down and against the sides with a piece of the dough, *not* with the fingers. Place a piece of paper in each form and fill up with grains of corn (this is only to prevent them from puffing up). Set aside to cool for 20 mins. before baking them light and crisp in a fast oven. Remove corn and paper. Can be kept in an air-tight tin for later use.

PARTY CAKES

The following 7 cakes are all variations on a theme. They are all very small—we like to call them 'heavenly mouthfuls'. As each has its own individual taste and appearance, it is a good idea to bake just a few of each and arrange them together on a plate. They will look so attractive and decorative that your guests will want to try every one. (See color photograph on back cover — they are the ones on the round wooden platter, left center.

The recipe is only given in full for the first cake; for the six that follow, only the variations in the preparation of the butter cream and in the decoration are described.

33. RUM TOPS
Romtoppe

(makes approx. 25)

1 layer of layer-cake pastry (77)
buttercream (22)
rum
sugar icing (44)
cocktail cherries

Take a layer of pastry and cut out into round cookie shapes with a wineglass. Stir rum (according to taste) into buttercream until a smooth mass is obtained—can be warmed a little if necessary. Put mixture in a pastry tube with a smooth tip. Squirt out a little on the top of each cake. Place in refrigerator until stiff. Warm icing slightly. Place in greaseproof paper funnel and squirt over the cold cakes. Decorate each with a cocktail cherry. When squirting the icing it is best to place the cakes on a rack.

34. LEMON TOPS
Citrontoppe

(makes approx. 25)

1 layer of pastry (77)
buttercream (22)
1 lemon
sugar icing (44)
cooking chocolate

As for 33, but mix the juice and grated rind of 1 lemon into the buttercream. Color icing yellow. Place a little melted chocolate in a greaseproof paper funnel and decorate cakes with very thin stripes.

35. CHOCOLATE TOPS
Chokoladetoppe

(makes approx. 25)

1 layer of pastry (77)
buttercream (22)
cocoa
sugar icing (44)
walnuts or »gold-dust«

As for 33, but this time stir a little cocoa into the buttercream until it tastes good and looks good. Add a little cocoa to the icing as well. Decorate with "gold-dust" or halved walnuts.

36. RASPBERRY TOPS
Hindbærtoppe

(makes approx. 25)

1 layer of pastry (77)
buttercream (22)
raspberry jam
sugar icing (44)
candied violets or »gold-dust«

As for 33. Stir raspberry jam into the buttercream. Color icing red. Decorate with candied violets or "gold-dust"

37. MOCHA TOPS
Moccatoppe

(makes approx. 25)

1 layer of pastry (77)
buttercream (22)
mocha essence or soluble coffee
sugar icing (44)
cooking chocolate

As for 33, but this time stir mocha essence or soluble coffee into the buttercream, also a little in the icing.

Place a little melted chocolate in a greaseproof paper funnel and decorate with a "snail" twist.

38. HAZELNUT TOPS
Nøddetoppe

(makes approx. 25)

1 layer of pastry (77)
buttercream (22)
hazelnuts
sugar icing (44)
rum

As for 33. Chop the hazelnuts finely and stir into the buttercream with a little rum. Color icing pale green. Place half a hazelnut on the top of each cake.

39. HALF MOONS
Halvmåner

(makes approx. 25)

1 layer of pastry (77)
buttercream (22)
sugar icing (44)
raspberry jam or other jam
cocktail cherries

Cut the pastry into strips about 1¼ ins. wide. Spread half of the strips first with raspberry jam and then with a layer of buttercream. Sandwich the remaining half of the strips on top. Cut into halfmoons (or just squares for the sake of simplicity) and decorate with different colored icing. Place a cocktail cherry on the top of each cake.

40. MARZIPAN
Kransekagemasse

2 cups sweet almonds
6-8 bitter almonds
2 cups powdered sugar
2 whites of egg

Our wedding and birthday cakes are nearly always towering edifices of solid marzipan; for, next to whipped cream, marzipan is probably what we enjoy sinking our teeth into most. Wedding and birthday cakes are seldom attempted by the Danish house-wife, but Marzipan Cakes (41) and Hans Andersen Cakes (42) are comparatively easy to make.

Scald almonds (do not boil), peel and soak in water for a couple of hours until blanched. Dry thoroughly and put them twice through the grinder. Mix with sugar and the whites of egg. Toast slowly over low heat for about 20 mins.

41. MARZIPAN CAKES
Kransekager

marzipan (40)
2-3 whites of egg

¾ cup powdered sugar
½ cup sugar
1 tablespoon flour
pinch of salt of hartshorn
white icing (45)

Mix all the ingredients well together. Toast the mass slowly in a pot until it begins to stick to the bottom. Roll into long round ropes about the thickness of your finger and the length of your baking sheet. *Grease baking sheets* and place the strips on them. Press along the edges with the fingers so that they become narrow and pointed along the top and broad at the base. Bake in moderate oven (preferably with one empty sheet below) until very pale golden. When cold, glaze with white icing (45) by placing the icing in a greaseproof paper funnel and cutting a little bit of the tip off, so that the icing is squirted out in a very thin stream by squeezing the funnel. Pass quickly back and forth over the strips in a zigzagging movement. When the icing is dry, cut the strips into suitable lengths. Alternatively they can be formed into rings before baking, whereafter finish off in same way.

42. HANS ANDERSEN CAKES
H. C. Andersen kager

(makes approx. 40)

marzipan (40)
stiff apple jam
green coloring
rum
chocolate icing (44)
dough as for *Medals* (17)
walnuts

It is not so hard to see how these little gems got their name. First of all, nobody can deny that the recipe shows imagination, and secondly, you'll find that both children and grown-ups are enchanted by them! Roll out dough and cut into round shapes with a wineglass. Bake pale golden. Work marzipan and apple jam together, equal parts of each. Add a little green coloring and rum. Place in pastry tube and squirt on to the cake bases. Dip the top of each cake in thin chocolate icing, previously heated to approx. 95°. Decorate each with half a walnut.

43. VANILLA CUSTARD
Vanillecreme

2 cups milk or cream
2 tablespoons sugar
2 teaspoons flour
vanilla
2 whole eggs
1 yolk of egg

Boil the milk together with the vanilla. Beat eggs, sugar and flour until white—the longer you beat the better. Add a little of the boiling milk to the egg-sugar-flour mixture. Pour the lot into the rest of the milk and bring to the boil again, stirring constantly. The custard must be stirred now and again while cooling off as otherwise a skin will form on top.

44. SUGAR ICING
Glasur

3 cups powdered sugar
3 tablespoons boiling water

Sift sugar. Stir into the water until a smooth mass is obtained. Color and taste can be varied by mixing in lemon, cocoa, etc., etc.

45. WHITE ICING
Æggehvideglasur

1 white of egg
½ cup powdered sugar (approx.)
a few drops of vinegar

Sift the sugar and stir in the white of egg and vinegar until the mass becomes white and stiff and does not run; it may be necessary to add a little more powdered sugar. Especially good for squirting on the tops of cakes in decorative form. Can be colored if desired.

DANISH PASTRY,
BUNS, ROLLS & BREAD

DANISH PASTRY
Wienerbrød

Out of deference to the English-speaking world we have quite happily agreed to the use of the term "Danish Pastry" to describe the goodies which decorate half the shelves in the windows of every single baker's shop throughout Denmark. Among ourselves however, we call it "Viennese Bread", which seems to puzzle a few of our visitors. Quite frankly, we are happy to let them go on being puzzled and not delve too deeply into the matter, for there is a risk of somebody digging up evidence to the effect that it was some master baker in Vienna who thought up the recipe before we did. On the other hand, whenever people tactlessly start murmuring about this possibility, we comfort ourselves with the fact that the Germans and Austrians sensibly call the stuff "Copenhagen Pastry".

People say these pastries are fattening.

They are.

46. DOUGH for DANISH PASTRY

Wienerbrødsdejg

(enough for approx. 45 pastries)

1 cup cold milk
2 oz. yeast
¼ cup sugar
2 eggs
2 cups *margarine* or butter
5 cups flour
1 egg for brushing
½ cup flour to roll dough in

Work the yeast, sugar and eggs together with the fingers in the milk, then sift in the 5 cups flour. Knead until you have a dough that slides smoothly in the hands. Sprinkle the table with flour and place the dough on it. This pastry turns out better with margarine, but butter can of course be used instead. Form the margarine into a square and place on top of the dough. Pack the dough up over the margarine to form a square again and roll out to a rectangle about ½ in. thick. Fold inwards a third from one end and another third from the other end over on top of the first so that the dough is in three layers. The dough has now been rolled *once*. Repeat *twice more* in exactly the same way. Set to cool for 15 mins. Cut into four equal pieces and you now have sufficient dough to make about 45 pastries, 10–12 of each of 4 different varieties.

47. "SPANDAUERS"

Spandauer

(makes approx. 10)

1 piece of "Viennese Bread" dough (46)
raspberry jam
or vanilla custard (43)
chopped nuts
sugar icing (44)

Roll the dough out to a rectangle about 20 ins. long by 6 ins. wide. Cut down lengthways into two strips. Cut each strip into 5 equal parts, thus forming a total of 10 squares of dough. Fold in the four corners of each towards the center and press down well. Place on baking sheet with plenty of space between each. Brush with egg. Place a dot of raspberry jam *or* vanilla custard in the middle of each and sprinkle with a few chopped nuts. Set aside to rise for about 15 mins. Bake in moderate oven until golden brown and crisp. When cold, spread a teaspoonful of sugar icing on each. Just one tip that applies to all variations of "Viennese Bread": eat them as oven-fresh as possible, for they were never designed to be kept in a tin, no matter how airtight!

48. "TRIANGLES"
Trekanter

(makes approx. 10)

1 piece of "Viennese Bread" dough (46)
pastry filling (55)
chopped nuts
egg for brushing
sugar icing (44)

Roll out dough and cut into 10 squares as for *Spandauers* (47). Put a dot of pastry filling (55) in the center of each square and fold over, forming a triangle. Press the two edges well together and make about 5–6 slashes in each with a knife. Brush with egg (previously well beaten up) and sprinkle a few chopped nuts in the middle. Place on baking sheet and allow to rise for about 15 mins. Bake in moderate oven until golden brown and crisp. When cold, spread a teaspoon of sugar icing on the top of each.

49. "CREAM BUNS"
Cremeboller

(makes approx. 10)
1 piece of "Viennese Bread"
　　dough (46)
vanilla custard (43)
powdered sugar

Roll out dough and cut into 10 squares as for *Span-dauers* (47). Squirt a blob of vanilla custard about the size of a walnut in the center of each. Fold in the four corners towards the center around the custard. Place on baking sheet with folds facing *downwards*. Press lightly on top and brush with egg. Allow to rise for about 15 mins. and then bake in a moderate oven until golden brown. When cold, sprinkle with powdered sugar.

50. & 51. "SCRUBBING BRUSHES" and "COMBS"
Skrubber og Kamme

(makes 10-12 of each)
2 pieces of "Viennese Bread"
　　dough (46)
pastry filling (55)
sugar
chopped nuts

Roll out the two pieces of dough as for *Span-dauers* (47) but *do not cut until later*. On each spread a good layer of pastry filling (55) down the middle with a spatula. Fold one side (about ⅓ of the width) over on top of the filling and brush with a little egg. Then fold the other side over on top of the first, so that you have a long strip in three layers. Press lightly so that it holds together. Turn upside down and brush with egg on the *smooth* side. Mix a little sugar and chopped nuts in a plate.

"*Scrubbing Brushes*" are now made with one of the pieces. Cut the piece into 10–12 pastries, making

the cuts slightly diagonally across. Dip in the sugar-
nut mixture. Place on baking sheet. To make "*Combs*"
cut the second piece similarly into 10–12 smaller
pieces and make 5–6 slashes down one side of each
with a knife. Place on oven sheet. Allow all the
pastries to rise for about 15 mins. and bake in a
moderate oven until golden brown and crisp.

52. "APPLE COMBS" (or "COCKSCOMBS")
Æblekamme eller Hanekamme

(makes approx. 10)
1 piece of "Viennese Bread" dough (46)
apple jam
chopped nuts
sugar icing (43)

Roll out and cut dough into 10 squares as for *Span-
dauers* (47). Place a teaspoonful of apple jam in the
center of each. Fold over once across the middle
and press the two edges well together. Make 5–6
slashes in this edge with a knife. Place on baking
sheet and brush with egg. Sprinkle with a few
chopped nuts. Allow to rise for about 15 mins. Bake
in moderate oven until golden brown. When cold,
spread a teaspoonful of sugar icing on each.

53. BIRTHDAY SUGAR PRETZEL
Fødselsdagskringle

1 piece of "Viennese Bread" dough (46)

pastry filling (55)
vanilla custard (43)
raisins
candied peel
chopped nuts
sugar
1 egg for brushing

Roll out dough about 24 ins. in length by 4 ins.
wide. Down the middle spread a thin layer of pastry

filling (55) with a spatula. On top of this spread a thin layer of vanilla custard and sprinkle with raisins and candied peel. Fold one side (about ⅓ of the width) over on top of the filling, then the other third on top of this. Turn the whole pastry upside down. Place on baking sheet and form into giant pretzel shape. Brush with egg. Sprinkle with chopped nuts and sugar. Allow to rise approx. 15 mins. Bake golden brown and crisp in moderate oven.

54. DANISH COFFEE RING

Smørkage

(serves 4 persons)
⅓ cup cold milk
½ oz. yeast (slightly over)
1 tablespoon sugar

1 egg
½ cup butter
½ or 1 cup flour
1 egg for brushing
pastry filling (55)
vanilla custard (43)
raisins
sugar icing (44)
a few chopped almonds

To make this delicious pastry-cake you need a round cake form about the size of a plate. In theory the recipe should serve 4 persons, but if two people are left to tackle it by themselves there is seldom much left either.

Make the pastry in the same way as for No. 46. When the dough has been rolled out for the last time, grease the inside of the form with butter. Roll out *one third* of the dough to about ½ in. thickness and line the form with it. Roll out the rest of the dough approx. 12 ins. long by 9 ins. wide. On top of this spread first a layer of pastry filling, then a

OPPOSITE: *top left: Cream Buns (49) and "Scrubbing Brushes" (50); in basket, from top: Plaited Rolls (63), Salt Finger Rolls (62), Rolls (60), Horns (61); bottom left: Tea Horns (65); bottom right: "Triangles" (48), "Spandauers" (47) and "Combs" (51).*

layer of vanilla custard and finally sprinkle a layer of raisins over the lot. Roll up lengthways. Go back to the cake form and spread a thin layer of vanilla custard on top of the pastry. Slice the roll into 10 slices. Place one in the middle of the form and group the rest round it in a circle. Brush them with egg and sprinkle with a few chopped almonds.

Place somewhere fairly warm to rise for about 20 mins. Bake in a moderate oven for about 25 to 30 mins.

When cool, remove from form and glaze each of the ten little 'rings' with sugar icing.

55. PASTRY FILLING
Remonce

½ cup butter
½ cup sugar
vanilla

Cream sugar and butter. Stir in vanilla and the filling is ready for use.

BUNS, ROLLS & BREAD

We seem to have an enormous number of recipes in Denmark for things which become extraordinarily tasty provided you spread a little butter on them. Seeing that good butter is one thing from which we Danes decidedly suffer no shortage, perhaps this is not surprising! A whole book would be necessary to cover *all* the recipes in this category, but here, at any rate, are a few of the most popular.

56. CURRANT BUNS

Teboller

(makes approx. 30)

½ cup cold milk
1 oz. yeast
2 tablespoons sugar
1 egg
½ cup butter
2 cups flour
½ cup raisins
1 egg for brushing

Nothing so very Danish about these—just buns. But as buns go, they're good buns!

Work egg, yeast, sugar and milk together with the fingers. Sift in flour and add raisins. Knead well until you have a dough that slides smoothly in the hands. Form into 30 equal-sized buns. Place on baking sheet. Press lightly and brush with egg. Allow to rise for about 20 mins. Bake golden brown in a good fast oven.

57. CARNIVAL BUNS

Fastelavnsboller

(makes approx. 10)
1 piece of "Viennese Bread" dough (46)
raisins
chopped candied peel
a little sugared water

Our Shrovetide celebrations consist mainly in antics round a barrel in which we pretend there is a cat (in olden times there was a cat) and in using the occasion as a good excuse for a bit of serious cake-eating. We like to eat these buns to replenish all the energy expended on the cat and the barrel—but even if you can't supply this local color we think you'll like them anyway!

Roll out dough and cut as for *Spandauers* (47). In the middle of each square of dough drop a few raisins and chopped candied peel. Fold in the four corners towards the center. Place on baking sheet with the four corners facing *downwards*. Press well. Brush with egg. Set aside to rise for about 15 mins. and bake until golden brown in moderate oven. Remove from oven when done and brush with a little sugared water.

The filling in these buns can be varied and they can also be glazed with differently colored icings. Otherwise same procedure as above. These buns are always eaten at carnival time in Denmark.

58. CHRISTMAS CAKE
Julekage

(makes 2 cakes)
½ cup milk
½ cup margarine
½ cup raisins
2⅔ cups flour
1 egg
1 tablespoon yeast
1½ tablespoons sugar
grated rind and juice of 1
   lemon

This must be just about the plainest recipe boasting the name of "Christmas Cake" in the world. But try it, and we think you'll find that it proves that a cake doesn't have to consist of 90% exciting dried fruits in order to be good!

Mix all the ingredients into a dough. Divide into two round clumps and flatten. Brush topsides with egg. Allow to rise for 15 mins. Baking time: approx. ½ hour in good hot oven.

59. LUNCHEON ROLL DOUGH

Kuvertbrødsdejg

(makes approx. 30)

⅓ cup milk

1 oz. yeast
½ tablespoon sugar
½ teaspoon salt
¼ cup butter
1⅔ cups flour
1 egg

Warm milk. Work the yeast, sugar, salt and egg into the milk with the fingers. When yeast has dissolved, sift in flour and knead into a dough that slides easily in the hands. Sprinkle with a little flour and wrap up in a clean cloth. Set aside to rise for about 20 mins. in a warm place. Press dough well to remove air and it is then ready to make any of the variations given below.

60. ROLLS

Rundstykker

(makes approx. 30)
dough (59)
1 egg for brushing

Roll dough into three equal-sized sausage shapes, divide each again into 10 pieces. Form each of the 30 pieces of dough into a slightly oblong bun. Place on baking sheet and brush with egg. Allow to rise for roughly 15 mins. Bake in a fast oven until they are pale and crisp on the outside.

61. HORNS

Horn

(makes approx. 30)
dough (59)
1 egg for brushing

Roll dough and divide into 30 pieces as for No. 60. Form each into an oblong bun shape and then roll them out with a rolling pin into ovals about 4½ ins. long. Press one end together into a small clump and then roll the dough up tightly round it with the fingers. Twist the ends round to form a crescent shape. Place on baking sheet and brush with egg. Allow to rise for about 15 mins. and bake in a fast oven until pale and crisp on the outside.

62. SALT FINGER ROLLS
Saltstænger

(makes approx. 35)
dough (59)
1 egg for brushing
salt

Divide dough into 7 equal parts. Roll each into a long rope about the length of your baking sheet. Place on baking sheet and brush with egg. Sprinkle a *little* coarse salt along the top of each rope. Allow to rise for about 10 mins. Bake golden crisp in a good fast oven. When done, cut each rope into 5 equal lengths. Served especially with all soups.

63. PLAITED ROLLS
Fletninger

(makes approx. 30)
dough (59)
1 egg for brushing

If you happen to have a long-haired daughter at home you can practise on before attempting these plaited rolls, so much the better. If not, just take your time and do your best. The result is almost certain to be decorative in one way or another.

Roll and divide dough into 30 pieces as for No. 60. Halve each piece so that you have 60. Roll each into a rope about 6 or 7 ins. long. Take two of the "ropes" and lay one over the other in the form of a cross.

Press in the middle so that they stick together. Take two opposite ends and cross them over each other, then take the other two ends and cross them over the first two. Continue to plait upwards from the table until you have used up the "ropes". Plait all the dough in the same manner. Place on baking sheet, brush with egg and allow to rise for about 15 mins. Bake until light and crisp in a fast oven.

64. WHITE BREAD
Franskbrød

(makes 1 loaf)

½ cup milk
1 oz. yeast (shade over)
1 egg
4 teaspoons sugar
1 teaspoon salt
2⅔ cups flour
egg for brushing

In Denmark we call this, our most popular form of white loaf, a "French" loaf. The French disclaim all responsibility, but we like the name anyway. It seems we have a marked aversion against formally denominating anything we make, good or bad, as "Danish". An exception is our bottled aerated water, which we proudly call "Danish Water". But seeing that both the ingredients (air and water) are indisputably Danish, nobody has ever held it against us.

Warm milk slightly. Work yeast, sugar, salt and egg together into the milk. Sift in flour and knead well until the dough slides easily in your hands. Sprinkle with a little flour and wrap in a clean cloth. Put aside in a warm place for about 20 mins. Press air out well and form into an oblong, rounded loaf, slightly flattened on the bottom. Place on baking sheet, brush with egg and allow to rise for 15 mins. Brush with egg once again. Bake in a fast oven for 20 to 25 mins.

65. TEA HORNS
Tehorn

(makes approx. 30)
½ cup milk
1 small egg

½ cup powdered sugar
¾ cup butter
1 oz. baking powder (just under)
3 cups flour
egg for brushing
crystalized sugar

Work butter, powdered sugar, baking powder, milk and the egg together with the fingers. Sift in flour and knead into a smooth dough. Place on a board and pat into a flat square. Place in refrigerator for about 30 mins. until it is stiff. Cut into two rectangular pieces. Roll each piece out about 20 ins. long by 6 ins. wide. Cut each piece into 15 triangular shapes and roll these up with the fingers from the base towards the apex. Place on baking sheets, 15 on each. Brush with egg and sprinkle with crystalized sugar. Put in a hot oven immediately and bake pale and crisp on the outside.

Section 4

LOAF CAKES & LAYER CAKES

LOAF CAKES

Loaf cakes have the advantages of being easy to bake and easy to keep. For this reason they are enormously popular in Denmark. The most popular of all is *Sandcake* (68). Everybody in Denmark eats sandcake, everybody bakes it and it is sold not only by all bakers and confectioners, but also by all grocers, all dairies and even, it is claimed, by a certain number of enterprising greengrocers. It rears its fluffy yellow head on the service counters of all railway station restaurants, all coffee bars and all village tea-shops. Despite its somewhat uninspired name it can be very, very good, even the railway station variety, which is saying something. Of course it all depends on how much butter and how many eggs you use, and how long you beat. Our grandmothers vented their wrath on kitchen-maids who beat for less than one solid hour and they turned their noses up at recipes calling for less than 12 eggs. But then of course we didn't export so many eggs in those days as we do now.

Export or no export, one of the recipes in this

section (76) bravely demands 14 eggs. This is not a misprint. By modern standards and notions of cake-baking it may sound a lot of eggs, but we can assure you that the resultant cake is well worth every single one of them!

66. SODA CAKE
Sodakage

½ cup butter
1 cup sugar
3 cups flour
5 eggs, separated
1 cup milk
grated rind of 1 lemon
1 teaspoon baking soda
2 teaspoons cream of tartar
pinch of salt

Cream butter and sugar until white. Stir in egg yolks, grated lemon rind and salt. Sift flour together with baking soda and cream of tartar and stir in with the milk. Finally add stiffly beaten egg whites. Grease a cake pan with butter and sprinkle with flour. Tip dough into pan and bake in a hot oven for about 1 hour.

67. JAM ROLL
Roulade

⅔ cup butter
1 cup sugar
5 eggs
2 cups flour
1 teaspoon salt of hartshorn
raspberry jam

If you have been studying this book at all carefully, you will have noticed by now that we Danes have a great weakness for raspberry jam. In nearly all our national recipes that call for jam, we are inclined to feel that it *must* be raspberry. In this case however, we have to confess that practically any jam will do just as well.

Cream butter and sugar until white. Stir in eggs one at a time. Stir well between each egg so that the batter gets light and fluffy. Sift in flour and salt of hartshorn. Mix thoroughly. Cover two baking sheets with thin paper. Divide the batter between the two, spreading it out in a square on each, about ½ in. thick. Bake pale golden in moderate oven. Spread two more pieces of paper on your table and sprinkle them with a thin layer of sugar. When the two squares are done, turn them on to the papers sprinkled with sugar, topside down, and remove the papers on which they were baked. Spread a thin layer of raspberry jam on each and roll up the cakes lightly. Wrap the paper round them and *do not remove* until they have cooled.

68. SANDCAKE
Sandkage

1 cup butter *or* margarine
1 ¼ cups sugar
1 ⅔ cups wheaten flour
6 eggs (separated)
vanilla

Cream butter and sugar in a bowl. Stir in egg yolks one at a time. Sift in flour and mix thoroughly. Finally fold in the stiffly beaten egg whites. Line a cake pan with thin paper and fill up with the batter. Bake in a slow oven for about 1 hour 20 mins.

69. SISTER CAKE

Søsterkage

2 cups flour
½ cup butter
2 eggs

1 tablespoon sugar
1 oz. cup yeast
½ milk
½ teaspoon salt
½ cup raisins
¼ cup finely chopped candied
  peel

Warm milk slightly. Work butter, sugar, salt, yeast and eggs into the milk with the fingers. Work in flour, raisins and candied peel. Place dough somewhere warm for 30 mins. Form into a roll and place in a greased cake pan. Bake in moderate oven for about 30 mins. When done, turn out and sprinkle with powdered sugar.

70. BISCUIT CAKE

(does not require baking)

Chokoladekikskage

1 cup shortening
2 cups powdered sugar
1 cup cocoa
3 eggs
1 pack square biscuits
a little grated orange peel
a few almonds for decoration

Beat up eggs. Sift powdered sugar together with the cocoa and add to the eggs, stirring well. Stir in grated orange peel. Melt shortening slightly and pour in, stirring continuously. Take a rectangular, deep cake pan, grease with butter and line with paper. Fill up with alternate layers of cocoa-sugar-egg mixture and biscuits, beginning and finishing up with the cocoa mixture. Place somewhere cool. When it has cooled, the cake can easily be tapped out of the form. Remove paper and decorate on top with a few peeled almonds.

71. TEA CAKE
Tekage

1 cup butter
1 ½ cups sugar
2 eggs

3 ½ cups flour
1 cup milk
¾ cup currants
¼ cup candied peel
1 teaspoon crushed cloves
1 teaspoon crushed cinnamon
1 teaspoon baking soda

Soften butter and stir in sugar. Cream until white and fluffy. Stir in eggs one at a time. Sift flour, cloves, cinnamon and baking soda together and then add in the currants and finely chopped candied peel. Place in bowl and tip in the butter-sugar-egg mixture. Finally stir in the milk. Place in greased cake pan and bake in cool oven for about 90 mins.

72. MOCHA CAKE
Moccakage

¾ cup butter
1 cup sugar

4 eggs
1 ½ cups flour
½ cup peeled and grated almonds
mocha cream filling (73)

Cream butter and sugar until white. Stir in eggs one at a time. Sift in flour and grated almonds. Tip batter into a round, greased cake pan. Bake in moderate oven for about 80 mins. When cold, cut into two layers. Spread mocha cream filling in between and on top for decoration.

73. MOCHA CREAM FILLING
Moccacreme

½ cup butter
1 cup powdered sugar
1 egg
2 teaspoons soluble coffee powder

Cream butter and powdered sugar until smooth and fluffy. Stir in egg and finally the *dry* coffee powder.

74. NOUGAT CAKE

Nougatkage

½ cup butter
1½ cups powdered sugar
3 eggs

3½ cups flour
1 cup milk
2 teaspoons salt of hartshorn
1 lemon
buttercream (22)
hard nougat (110)

Cream butter and powdered sugar until white. Stir in eggs one at a time. Add grated rind and juice of 1 lemon. Sift flour and salt of hartshorn together and stir in together with the milk. Place batter in a round, greased cake pan and bake in fairly hot oven for about 60 mins. When the cake has cooled, cut into three layers and spread buttercream between them. Spread a thin layer of buttercream on the sides of the cake and finally sprinkle the crushed hard nougat all over.

75. HONEY CAKE

Honningkage

1 cup honey *or* sirup
1¼ cups sugar
½ cup water

1½ teaspoons baking soda
2 eggs
1 teaspoon crushed cinnamon
1 teaspoon crushed ginger
1 teaspoon crushed cloves
a little chopped orange peel
4 cups wheaten flour

This is a very old Danish recipe. Danish children have for many generations had a weakness for honey cake, a fact confirmed by Hans Andersen in more than one of his fairy-tales!

Warm the honey, sugar and water in a pot, *but do not allow to boil*. When cool, stir in the baking powder, previously dissolved in a little water, and the two eggs, beaten together. Add cinnamon, ginger, cloves and the finely chopped orange peel. Finally sift in flour and mix the lot thoroughly. Tip the batter into two greased and floured cake pans and bake in a slow oven for about 1 hour. When the cakes have cooled, either cut into slices and butter, or cut into two layers and spread buttercream in between.

76. NUT CAKE
Nøddekage

14 eggs, separated
2½ cups sugar
2½ cups finely grated hazel-
　　nuts

Cream the yolks well with the sugar. Stir in hazel-nuts. Fold in the stiffly beaten egg whites. Place in deep, rectangular form, Bake in cool oven for 40 to 50 mins. Decorate with whipped cream if you absolutely must!

LAYER CAKES

The principal of layer cakes is extremely simple. In Denmark we like the 3-layer variety, but there is nothing to stop anyone using either 2 or 4 layers according to fancy. The filling between the layers can also be varied endlessly, likewise the icing and decoration on top. The recipe given here, (No. 78) is a fairly "standard" example. Keen students of Danish home baking practice should observe that here again, we still remain faithful to our beloved raspberry jam!

77. PASTRY for LAYER CAKES

Lagkagebunde
(makes 6 layers)

⅔ cup butter
1 cup sugar
5 eggs
2 cups flour
1 teaspoon salt of hartshorn

Cream butter and sugar until white. Stir in eggs one at a time. Mix thoroughly. Sift flour together with the salt of hartshorn and stir in. Divide into six clumps and spread out evenly on six round pieces of greaseproof paper each about the size of a plate. Bake in a fast oven. When done, remove from baking sheet straight away. *Leave paper on* until pastry is required.

78. ICING LAYER CAKE

Lagkage med glasur

3 layers of pastry (77)
vanilla cream (43)
icing (44)
raspberry jam
a few chopped almonds

This is the "simplified" version, eaten as cake, of the Cream Layer Cake (80) exalted to the category of dessert.

Remove paper from pastry layers. On the first spread a layer of raspberry jam and on top of this a layer of vanilla cream. Cover with second layer of pastry. Spread a layer of vanilla cream on this and finally place the last layer of pastry on top. Glaze with icing and sprinkle with a few chopped almonds while the icing is still soft.

Section 5

DESSERTS

Few of our favorite desserts require baking in an oven, so strictly speaking they do not fall under the title of "Danish Home Baking". On the other hand many of them make use of a number of the same ingredients we use in our cakes—just handled and dressed up differently. After all, half the art (and the fun) of preparing food is ringing variations.

Some may be new to you, some may not. Far be it from us to suggest that you have never explored the mysteries of stewed rhubarb, stewed gooseberries, pancakes or rice fritters. But we include these too because there is always the possibility that the way we like to make these desserts is not quite the same as the way you have been accustomed to. If you like our way, well and good. If you think your own way is better, than at least you will have satisfied your curiosity concerning this department of the Danish cuisine and can set your mind at rest in the knowledge that you haven't missed anything after all. But don't discard some of the more common-place looking recipes too quickly—have you ever tried, for instance, adding a little beer to the batter when making Apple Fritters?

The first three desserts in this section are big brothers to the small Napoleon Cakes (25). Sometimes you can hardly see them for the whipped cream. Strangely enough, a slice of any one of these cakes is not really as filling as it looks. If you were a little mouse and spent a couple of hours creeping round the tables of a Danish coffee-shop, either morning or afternoon, you might be surprised to observe with what comparative ease most Danish girls between the ages of 5 and 85 manage to put away two and even three slices at one sitting. And somehow or other the whipped cream seldom seems to show on Danish figures (male or female) until we reach 40 or so, when it certainly does. But this does not really worry us, for after about 200 years of practice we find that good humor often increases proportionately with girth.

79. NAPOLEON CAKE (large and round)
Napoleonskage

(serves about 8 persons)
puff paste (24)
vanilla custard (43)
icing (44)
raspberry jam
2 cups whipping cream

This dessert should be served (and the same applies to the two that follow, Nos. 80 and 81) only at festive dinner parties and banquets when there is a reasonable hope that there will be some speech-making in between the main meat course and the dessert. And if, contrary to the normal course of events (in Denmark) the speeches should be very short, it is advisable to start off with a fairly modest portion only—otherwise you may have cause for regret, which, seeing that this really is an emperor of a cake, would be a pity!

Roll out dough to roughly ¼ in. thickness and cut into three cake layers each about the size of a plate. Place on baking sheet and prick well with a fork. Let stand for approx. 30 mins. before putting in to bake until pale golden and crisp in a very moderate oven. When cool, take one of the layers, turn upside down so that the smooth side faces upwards, and glaze with icing. This will be the top layer of the cake. Then take a cake-plate and start building your cake up on it as follows: take another layer of pastry, and spread raspberry jam on it. On top of the jam spread a layer of vanilla custard. On top of the custard another layer of pastry. Cover this with whipped cream and finally put on the "lid", i.e. the layer previously glazed with icing. Press this top layer down *lightly* so that the whipped cream is squeezed out to the edge of the cake. Smooth off with a spatula.

80. CREAM LAYER CAKE *Flødelagkage*

(serves about 10 persons)
3 layers of pastry (77)

12 large macaroons
vanilla custard (43)
raspberry jam
2 cups whipping cream
canned fruit *or* hard jelly for decoration

Build up this layer cake as follows: layer of pastry, layer of raspberry jam, layer of vanilla custard, layer

of macaroons, thin layer of vanilla custard, layer of
pastry, thin layer of raspberry jam, layer of custard,
finally the last layer of pastry, topped off with a thin
layer of whipped cream. Put the rest of the whipped
cream in a pastry tube and squirt on to the cake as
artistically as you can. Decorate further with pieces
of canned fruit, hard jelly etc., according to taste. In
Denmark, on birthdays and other festive occasions,
we stick in tiny candles and little paper flags.

81. OTHELLO CAKE (serves about 10 persons)
Othellokage 3 layers of pastry (77)
vanilla custard (43)
12 macaroons
icing (44) flavored and colored
    with cocoa
2 cups whipping cream

Foreign visitors to Denmark, having visited Kron-
borg Castle and one or more of the 13 graves
scattered over the country purporting to contain
Hamlet's mortal remains, easily get the impression
that we Danes must be sadly ignorant of the fact that
Shakespeare also wrote one or two other things. It is
in an attempt to correct this unfortunate impression
that this cake has been given its present name.

Othello Cake is built up on a cake-plate as follows:
layer of pastry, layer of vanilla custard, layer of
macaroons, thin layer of vanilla custard, layer of
pastry; next, a thin layer of vanilla custard in which
a little whipped cream has been well mixed (this
layer should be thickest in the center of the cake,

forming a mound). Cover with the last layer of pastry, previously glazed with cocoa icing. Squirt the rest of the whipped cream round the sides.

82. RUM DELIGHT
Romfromage

(serves 8 persons)
5 eggs, separated
⅔ cup sugar
1 cup good rum
2 cups whipping cream
2 teaspoons powdered gelatine
(approx.)

Some say that if children are going to eat this dessert, rum essence should be used instead of real rum. But frankly, this would be sacrilege. Far better give the kids something else and enjoy the full-blooded version with your conscience at rest!

Cream yolks with powdered sugar. Stir in rum. Stir in whipped cream carefully, thereafter add the powdered gelatine, previously dissolved. Finally fold in stiffly beaten egg whites. Pour into a glass bowl and allow to cool. Decorate with whipped cream. In Denmark we like to serve a cold sweet fruit sauce, preferably red in color, with this dessert. See No. 108.

83. LEMON DELIGHT
Citronfromage

(serves 6 persons)
5 eggs, separated

¾ cup sugar
2 lemons
2 teaspoons powdered gelatine
(approx.)
1 cup whipping cream
hard jelly for decoration

The expression "melts in the mouth" is one often bandied about over-freely in cook-books. But if ever a dessert justified the label, this is it!

Cream yolks with sugar until white. Stir in grated rind of 1 lemon and juice of both. Add gelatine, previously dissolved. Fold in stiffly beaten egg whites. Stir the whole mass *carefully* until it begins to set, then tip into a glass bowl. Decorate with whipped cream and jelly.

84. PINEAPPLE DELIGHT *Ananasfromage*

(serves 6 persons)
10 eggs

¾ cup sugar
3 teaspoons powdered gelatine (approx.)
1 large can pineapple slices
2 lemons
2 cups whipping cream

Defies comment in prose. Try it and see!

Cream yolks with sugar until white. Dissolve gelatine and add into it the juice of the 2 lemons and the juice from the pineapple can. Slice pineapple into small pieces except for one ring, to be kept for final decoration. Put the pieces of pineapple into the creamed yolks together with the gelatine-juice mixture. Finally fold in the stiffly beaten egg whites. Tip into glass bowl. Decorate with whipped cream and the last pineapple ring.

85. CHOCOLATE PUDDING
Chokoladebudding

(serves 6 persons)
1 cup milk

½ cup sugar
4 egg yolks
4 oz. cooking chocolate
2 teaspoons powdered gelatine (approx.)
vanilla
2 cups whipping cream

Boil up milk together with half the sugar and the vanilla. Cream yolks with the rest of the sugar. Take off milk and stir in yolks carefully. Add the gelatine, previously dissolved. Break chocolate into small pieces, melt with a little hot water, and stir in. *Cool*, then fold in the whipped cream carefully. Serve in a glass bowl, together with custard (111) if desired.

86. EGG-AND-BREAD CAKE
Brødæggekage

(serves 3 persons)
6 slices white bread
4 eggs
1 tablespoon flour
½ teaspoon salt
1 cup milk

Melt a little butter in a pan, fry the 6 slices of bread lightly and remove. Whip up the flour in a little of the milk and then beat up the four eggs in this. Add salt and the rest of the milk. Melt a little butter in the pan again, pour in the batter and when it begins to stiffen, put the fried slices of bread in. Cook slowly until brown and crisp underneath. Turn out on a round dish with the bread downwards. Serve hot with sugar and jam to taste.

87. PANCAKES
Pandekager med syltetøj

(serves 4–5 persons)
1 ⅔ cups flour
¼ cup butter
2 cups milk
3 eggs
3 teaspoons sugar
½ teaspoon salt

If you want to gladden the heart of a Danish guest who is far from home, give him pancakes and rasp-berry jam. (But, to complete the nostalgia, you must also give him a first course of split pea soup served together with chunks of pork. The recipe for this dish is unfortunately beyond the scope of this book, but is to be found in "Danish Cookery" by Susanne).

Warm milk and stir in the sifted flour. Stir in a little melted butter, then the eggs, sugar, salt and lastly the rest of the melted butter. Pour the lot into a jug. Melt a *little* butter in a pan and pour in just a very little of the batter so that it spreads out evenly in a thin layer covering the whole of the bottom of the pan. Fry pale and crisp on both sides. If not fully confident of your ability to toss them, turn with a spatula—it may not be so exciting, but it is generally quicker in the long run. Serve as hot as possible with sugar and raspberry jam.

88. DOUGHNUTS
Æbleskiver

3½ cups flour
4 eggs
¼ cup sugar
3 cups milk
¼ cup butter
2 oz. yeast
a little crushed cardamom
grated rind of 1 lemon
½ teaspoon salt

(serves 8 persons)

In Denmark we call our doughnuts "Apple Slices", possibly because we think the best way to eat them is to slice them open and fill them with apple jam. To make them you require a special frying pan with 6 to 8 round indentations, (see photo opposite title-page).

Cream yolks and sugar until white. In another bowl, mix flour and milk. Add in the creamed yolks and sugar, thereafter melted butter, grated lemon rind, cardamom and salt. Finally add in the yeast, previously dissolved in a little warm milk. Mix the lot well and fold in the stiffly beaten egg whites. Set aside to rise for about 1 hour. Pour the batter into a jug. Put a little butter in each indentation and then pour in a little of the batter. They form into semi-spherical "shells", browned underneath, whereupon you turn them upside down with a knitting needle and brown on the other side, so that they close into hollow balls. Serve hot with sugar and jam to taste.

89. PANCAKES with ICECREAM
(serves 6 persons)

Pandekager med is

Same ingredients as for 87. Make these pancakes in a slightly smaller pan. When done on both sides, fold over in half, then fold once again. Put a lump of vanilla icecream in the top "pocket". Place on a dish and sprinkle with a thin layer of powdered sugar. Serve very quickly!

90. RICE FRITTERS
Risklatter

(serves 4 persons)
⅓ cup rice

2 cups milk
3 eggs, separated
3 tablespoons flour
2 teaspoons sugar
½ teaspoon salt
a little grated lemon rind

Cook the rice in the milk until done, then set aside to cool off. Then add the three *yolks*, flour, sugar, salt and grated lemon rind. Stir well. Fold in the stiffly beaten egg whites. Melt a little butter in the pan and drop in the batter by tablespoons. Fry golden brown on both sides. Serve hot with sugar and jam to taste.

91. PRINCESS RICE
Prinsesseris

(serves 6 persons)
⅓ cup rice
2 cups milk

vanilla
¼ cup sugar
1 cup whipping cream
¼ cup almonds
1 teaspoon powdered gelatine
  (approx.)

Cook rice in milk for about 1 hour, stirring frequently. When rice is done, add vanilla, sugar and gelatine (previously dissolved) also the peeled and chopped almonds. Warm the lot once more, then remove and set aside to cool, stirring now and again. When cool, fold in the whipped cream and tip into a glass bowl. Served with a red, cold, sweet fruit sauce (108) preferably with whole cherries floating in it.

92. RED FRUIT JELLY with CREAM
Rødgrød med fløde

(serves 10–12 persons)
1 lb. raspberries
1 lb. red currants
6 cups water
2½ cups sugar
½ cup almonds
1 cup sago flour

This is the famous Danish dessert whose claim to fame lies principally in the difficulty all foreigners encounter in pronouncing its Danish name, *Rødgrød med Fløde*. Translated literally it only means *Red*

Gruel with Cream, but it is really much more delicious than this somewhat uninspired name might suggest.

Rinse fruit. Place in a pot with the water and cook until all the juice is boiled out. Strain off juice, add sugar and bring to the boil again. When thoroughly cooked, remove, and add the sago flour, previously whipped up in a little water, stirring quickly the whole time. Pour into glass bowls, sprinkle with peeled and chopped almonds and set aside to cool. Serve with full cream.

93. STEWED RHUBARB
Rabarbergrød

(serves 5–6 persons)
1 lb. rhubarb
5 cups water
¾ cup sugar
½ cup corn starch
vanilla sugar

Rinse rhubarb and cut into 1-in. chunks. Boil them in the water until completely soft. Strain off juice and add sugar. Bring to the boil again and then remove. Add in the vanilla sugar and then the corn starch, previously stirred up in a little water. Stir quickly the whole time. Pour into a glass bowl and set aside to cool. Serve with sugar and cream.

94. STEWED GOOSEBERRIES
Stikkelsbærgrød

(serves 6 persons)
2 lbs. gooseberries
4 cups water
3 ½ cups sugar
½ cup corn starch
vanilla

Rinse, top and tail gooseberries, boil them in the water (in which sugar has first been dissolved) until soft and then remove from heat. Add vanilla, then the corn starch, previously mixed in a little water. Stir the whole time. Pour into a bowl and set aside to cool. Serve with sugar and cream.

95. APPLE TRIFLE
Æbletrifli

(serves 6–8 persons)

stewed apples
vanilla custard (43)
12 large macaroons *or* bread crumbs
1 ½ cups whipping cream
red currant jelly for decoration

Stew apples as for 96. Take a glass bowl and place in it firstly a layer of macaroons which have been previously softened in a little wine. (Alternatively, a layer of bread crumbs prepared as for 96). On top of the macaroons place a layer of stewed apples, then a layer of custard, and so on, layer for layer until you have used up all your ingredients. Decorate with whipped cream and red currant jelly.

96. APPLE CAKE
Æblekage

(serves 6–8 persons)

1 ½ lbs. apples
½ cup water
½ cup sugar (or according to taste)
½ cup bread crumbs
½ cup butter
1 ½ cups whipping cream
raspberry jam

This is delightfully easy to prepare at short notice. A variation is to use toasted oatmeal flakes instead of bread crumbs. Keep a supply ready toasted in an airtight tin.

Peel, core and chop apples. Boil them in the water

until soft. Add sugar (if desired) and remove from heat. Melt butter in a pan. Stir in the sugar and bread crumbs (previously mixed) and toast until lightly browned. Take a round cake form with a loose bottom and grease well with butter. Fill up with alternate layers of stewed apples, bread crumbs, and raspberry jam, ending up with a layer of apple. Press well together and turn out on a dish. Decorate with whipped cream. Alternatively, the cake can be baked in a moderate oven for about 30 mins. Allow to cool off and decorate with whipped cream.

97. BAKED APPLES
Indbagte æbler

(serves 6 persons)
12 large apples
puff paste (24)
cinnamon sugar
egg for brushing
1 cup whipping cream

A baked apple wrapped in pastry sounds quite filling. But in practice they seem to disappear very easily!

Peel and core apples. Roll puff paste out to a thickness of approx. ¼ in. and cut into squares big enough to fold up around each apple. Place each apple on a square of paste. Fill up hole in apple with cinnamon sugar. Pack the paste up round the apple. Turn upside down and place on baking sheet. Brush with beaten egg and sprinkle with a little sugar. Let stand about 15 mins. before putting in a fairly hot oven to bake until pastry is crisp. When cool, cut off tops with a sharp knife, decorate with a wreath of whipped cream and put the "lids" back on.

98. APPLE FRITTERS
Æbleringe

10 to 12 large apples
1 ½ cups flour
1 ½ cups milk
¼ cup sweet malt beer
1 egg
½ teaspoon salt
3 teaspoons sugar

(serves 6–8 persons)

Beat up egg with salt and sugar. Stir in first milk, then flour and finally add beer. Peel and core apples, then cut into slices about ¼ in. thick, forming rings. Dip the rings in the batter and drop into boiling oil or fat and cook golden brown on both sides. You will find a knitting needle the best implement to handle these rings when dipping in the batter, putting them in the oil, turning and taking out. Serve hot, sprinkled with a little powdered sugar.

99. CARAMEL RING
Karamelrand

(serves 8 persons)
8 yolks of egg
2 whole eggs
1 ¾ cups sugar
4 cups cream
vanilla
1 cup whipping cream

Cream yolks and the two whole eggs in 1 cup sugar. Stir the vanilla into the cream, bring to the boil and pour over the eggs *while actually boiling, stirring constantly.* Do not boil up again after this. Brown the rest of the sugar in a pan, stirring the whole time to avoid burning. Grease two ring forms with oil and spread the browned sugar in them. Pour the batter into the two forms. Put them in a deep oven dish filled with boiling water and place in oven for about

1 hour, until the puddings are stiff. Remove from oven and set aside to cool, *preferably* 24 hours. Turn them out on to a dish. Rinse forms with boiling water to make a sauce. When cool, mix up with the whipped cream and serve in a jug. Frozen cream can also be served if desired.

100. CREAM RING with STEWED FRUIT
Fløderand med henkogte frugter

(serves 6–8 persons)
3 eggs, separated
½ cup sugar
vanilla
2 cups whipping cream
2 teaspoons powdered gelatine (approx.)
stewed fruit

Cream yolks with sugar and vanilla. Whip up cream and fold stiffly beaten egg whites into it. Add gelatine, previously dissolved. Moisten the inside of ring form, sprinkle with sugar and pour in batter. Set aside to cool until stiff. Turn out on a dish and fill up the hole in the middle with various stewed fruits.

101. SNOWBALLS
Sneboller

(serves 6 persons)
1 cup water
½ cup butter
1 cup flour
4–5 eggs

Bring water and butter to the boil. When boiling, stir in flour and allow to cook through. Remove from heat and stir in eggs one at a time. Drop the batter by tablespoonfuls into boiling oil or fat. Cook until golden brown and take out with a perforated

spoon. Arrange on a dish and sprinkle with a thin
layer of powdered sugar. Serve with jam—preferably cowberry.

102. JAM OMELET
Omelet med marmelade

(serves 2 persons)
3 eggs
pinch of salt
1 teaspoon sugar
1 tablespoon cream
jam

Beat up eggs well. Add salt, sugar and cream. Melt
a little butter in a pan. Pour in batter and push with
a spatula so that it covers one half of the pan only.
When golden brown underneath, spread a thick
stripe of jam down the middle. Fold the two 'long'
sides over on top of the jam and turn out on a dish,
folds downwards. Sprinkle with sugar. Take a glow-
ing fork and burn the sugar to caramel. Serve as hot
as possible.

103. ORANGE OMELET
Appelsin-omelet

(serves 4–5 persons)
6 eggs
½ teaspoon salt
2 teaspoons sugar
2 teaspoons cream
2 oranges
grated hazelnuts

Proceed as for 102, but add the grated rind of the
oranges to the batter. Remove rest of the peel from
the oranges, cut the fruit into small pieces and mix
with the grated hazelnuts. Put this filling in the
omelet instead of jam and finish off in the same way.

104. VEILED COUNTRY LASS

Bondepige med slør

(serves 5 persons)
1 ½ cups crumbled rye bread
2 tablespoons sugar
2 tablespoons butter
1 lb. apples
raspberry jam
½ cup grated chocolate
1 cup whipping cream

It must be admitted that few country lasses wear veils these days, but when it comes to composing attractive names for attractive desserts, a little poetic licence has to be allowed. And at any rate, this country lass *has* a veil!

Stew apples as for 96. Melt butter in a pan. Mix crumbled rye bread and sugar together and tip into pan. Toast slowly until crisp. Take a glass bowl and place in it firstly a layer of the toasted rye bread, then a layer of raspberry jam, next a layer of stewed apples and finally a layer of grated chocolate. Continue building up in this way, layer for layer, ending up with a layer of bread. Decorate with whipped cream. On the top of the whipped cream sprinkle a fine 'veil' of grated chocolate.

105. WHIPPED CREAM CONES

Kræmmerhuse med flødeskum

(makes approx. 45)
3 eggs
powdered sugar (see below)
flour (see below)
1 tablespoon cold water
whipped cream
raspberry jam

Weigh eggs *with shells on* and take equal amount of powdered sugar plus equal amount of flour. Whip up eggs, powdered sugar and flour with an egg-whisk, thereafter add 1 tablespoon cold water. Grease cookie sheet. Take a coffeespoonful of the batter at a time and spread out thinly with a spatula on the sheet in the form of an oval. Bake until pale golden in moderate oven and form into cones by hand *while still warm* (otherwise they easily snap!). Keep in air-tight tin for later use. To serve, fill up each cone with whipped cream and decorate with raspberry jam.

106. DAMSON TART
Svedsketærte

(serves 8 persons)
puff paste (24)
stewed damsons (use ½ lb.
   stoned damsons)
2 cups whipping cream
1 egg for brushing

Roll out a piece of puff paste to a thickness of about ¼ in. Cut out a piece about the size of a plate and brush this round the edge with egg. Make an edging of puff paste about ³/₄ in. wide and press this on round the edge of the base. Place on baking sheet and prick well with a fork.

Take another piece of puff paste and cut into narrow strips about ½ in. wide. Place eight of these strips lengthways on a baking sheet about ½ in. apart. Brush these with egg. Take another eight strips and place across the first eight, also ½ in. apart, forming a network. Brush this top layer of strips with egg also. Cover with a plate and trim off round the edges with a knife so that you have a neat circle.

Brush with egg round the edge and press a strip of puff paste all round this edge. Set both the cake base and the network aside for about 20 mins. before placing in oven. Bake until light and crisp. When cool, spread a thick layer of stewed damsons in the base. On top of the damsons spread a thick layer of whipped cream. Sprinkle a little powdered sugar over the network top before placing it over the whipped cream, then press down lightly so that the whipped cream spreads out to the sides of the tart. Smooth off with a spatula. Add a little more stewed damson in the holes of the network—this is best done with a funnel of greaseproof paper.

107. VANILLA ICECREAM
Vanille is

(serves 8 persons)
3 yolks of egg
1 cup sugar
vanilla
3 cups whipping cream

Cream yolks with sugar until white. Stir in vanilla. Whip up cream and fold in. Moisten a form, pour in cream, and freeze.

108. SWEET FRUIT SAUCE
Frugtsauce

1 cup red fruit juice
1 cup water
¼ cup sugar
2 teaspoons corn starch

Add the water and sugar to the juice and bring to the boil. Thicken with corn starch previously stirred up in a very little water.

109. NOUGAT ICECREAM

(serves 8 persons)

Nougat is

Proceed as for 107 but stir in crushed hard nougat (110) instead of vanilla.

110. HARD NOUGAT

Hård nougat

2 cups powdered sugar
½ cup almonds
½ tablespoon butter

Scald, peel and chop almonds. Melt powdered sugar in a pan, stirring continuously. When melted and browned, add in first the butter and then the almonds. Grease a pan with butter and tip the mixture into it. When cold, crush. Keep in air-tight tin.

111. CUSTARD

Cremesauce

3 yolks of egg
½ cup sugar
2 teaspoons flour
1 teaspoon vanilla sugar
2 cups milk

Beat the eggs well with the sugar. Add in flour and vanilla sugar together with ½ cup of milk. Bring the rest of the milk to the boil and then pour in the batter. Bring the lot lightly to the boil once again and then pour into a bowl. Stir frequently while cooling off to avoid formation of skin.

112. CHOCOLATE ICECREAM

(serves 8 persons)

Chokolade is

Proceed as for 107 but stir in finely chopped cooking chocolate instead of vanilla.

Section 6

CHEESE CRACKERS

There is no real "cocktail hour" in Denmark, due largely to the fact that we have our dinners so early in the evening. What with coffee in the afternoon from about 3 o'clock to 4 o'clock, and dinner on the table already by about 6 o'clock, we just have neither time nor the energy to squeeze a cocktail session in between. The result is that most social drinking in Danish homes (apart, that is, from drinking at meal times) is indulged in *after* dinner. This has the undeniable advantage that one can take more alcohol on a full stomach than on an empty one.

As a nation, we are not great whisky or gin drinkers. This is not to say we don't like the stuff when we can get it. But the exorbitant purchase taxes on imported spirits put them beyond the means of the average Dane as daily fare.

In the evenings therefore, the older generation prefers coffee and a variety of sweet liqueurs of Danish origin, most of them very good and a few even of international repute. But the younger generation, not having such a sweet tooth, has begun to favor sherry or claret parties, preferably with lashings of one or the other, or both. Roast chestnuts are very popular on such occasions, and also cheesy titbits and crackers of various shapes and forms. These, apart from being tasty, augment thirst considerably and thus help any party to go with a swing.

113. CHEESE STRAWS
Ostestænger

(makes approx. 50)

1 cup butter
1⅔ cups flour
2 cups grated cheese (mild)
pinch of paprika
pinch of salt
1 egg for brushing

Mix the grated cheese together with the flour, salt and paprika. Work in the butter. Pat the dough into a rectangle and set aside to cool. When cold, roll out to roughly 24 ins. long by about 5 ins. wide. Brush with egg and sprinkle with grated cheese. Cut into approx. 50 straws. Place on a greased cookie sheet. Bake *very pale* golden. On no account allow to get browned as they will then taste bitter.

114. CHEESE MEDALLIONS
Ostemedaljer

(makes approx. 38)

1 cup butter
1⅔ cups flour
2 cups mild grated cheese
cream cheese (115)
green olives for
    decoration if desired

Mix grated cheese into the flour. Work in the butter. Set dough aside to cool for about 1 hour. Roll out, not too thin. Cut into cookie shapes with a wineglass and place on greased cookie sheets. Bake pale in slow oven. Are excellent just as they are, but as a variation can be placed two and two together with cream cheese spread in between. Squirt a dot of cream cheese on the top of each and decorate with a green olive.

115. CREAM CHEESE
Ostecreme

1 cup cream
½ cup grated cheese
2 egg yolks
2 teaspoons flour
pinch of salt
pinch of paprika

Beat the yolks together with the paprika, flour, salt and cream. Bring to the boil. As soon as the cream has thickened, remove from heat and whip in the grated cheese. Allow to cool.

116. CHEESE PIES
Ostelinser

(makes approx. 40)
dough as for 114
cream cheese (115)

Line very small cake forms with the dough. Fill up with cream cheese. Cut out "lids" of same dough and place on top, pressing firmly round the edge. Place on greased baking sheet and bake pale golden in slow oven.

117. SALTED PRETZELS
Saltkringler

(makes approx. 50)
luncheon roll dough (59)
2 egg yolks for brushing
salt

Roll dough into 5 long sausage shapes. Divide each into 10 equal parts. Roll each of these into thin ropes and form into pretzel shapes. Place on greased oven sheets. Brush with yolk of egg and sprinkle a little coarse salt over them. Set aside to rise for about 15 mins. Bake pale golden in a fast oven.

118. CHEESE PETITS-FOURS
Oste-petit-fours

equal parts butter and Roque-fort cheese
small round bases of white or brown bread
yellow, green and red coloring
radishes, paprika and walnuts for decoration

Soften butter and cheese in a pot, but *do not allow to melt*. Whip until smooth with an egg-whisk. Divide the mass into three portions. Add a *little* yellow coloring to the first, green to the second and red to the third. Squirt out on the tops of the bread bases and decorate with radishes, paprika and walnuts respectively.

119. CREAM CHEESE PUFFS
Vandbakkelser med ostecreme

(makes approx. 80)
puffs (19)
cream cheese (115)
grated cheese

Make these puffs very small. Fill with cream cheese by squirting it through the bottom (don't cut off the tops) using a pastry tube. Spread a little cream cheese on the top of each and dip in grated cheese.

WEIGHTS AND MEASURES

1 cup flour	=	$4^1/_2$ oz. or 125 grams
1 cup sugar	=	7 oz. or 200 grams
1 cup powdered sugar	=	$4^1/_2$ oz. or 125 grams
1 cup butter	=	$^1/_2$ lb. or 225 grams
1 cup almonds, chopped	=	$4^1/_2$ oz. or 125 grams
1 cup cocoa	=	$3^1/_2$ oz. or 100 grams
1 cup rice	=	7 oz. or 200 grams
4 cups coconut flour	=	$4^1/_2$ oz. or 125 grams
1 cup sirup	=	$10^1/_2$ oz. or 300 grams
1 cup liquid (milk etc.)	=	$2^1/_4$ decilitres

INDEX
English

NB: The numbers are recipe numbers, unless otherwise indicated.

Danish

A CATALOGUE OF SELECTED DOVER BOOKS
IN ALL FIELDS OF INTEREST

A CATALOGUE OF SELECTED DOVER BOOKS
IN ALL FIELDS OF INTEREST

AMERICA'S OLD MASTERS, James T. Flexner. Four men emerged unexpectedly from provincial 18th century America to leadership in European art: Benjamin West, J. S. Copley, C. R. Peale, Gilbert Stuart. Brilliant coverage of lives and contributions. Revised, 1967 edition. 69 plates. 365pp. of text.

21806-6 Paperbound $3.00

FIRST FLOWERS OF OUR WILDERNESS: AMERICAN PAINTING, THE COLONIAL PERIOD, James T. Flexner. Painters, and regional painting traditions from earliest Colonial times up to the emergence of Copley, West and Peale Sr., Foster, Gustavus Hesselius, Feke, John Smibert and many anonymous painters in the primitive manner. Engaging presentation, with 162 illustrations. xxii + 368pp.

22180-6 Paperbound $3.50

THE LIGHT OF DISTANT SKIES: AMERICAN PAINTING, 1760-1835, James T. Flexner. The great generation of early American painters goes to Europe to learn and to teach: West, Copley, Gilbert Stuart and others. Allston, Trumbull, Morse; also contemporary American painters—primitives, derivatives, academics—who remained in America. 102 illustrations. xiii + 306pp.

22179-2 Paperbound $3.00

A HISTORY OF THE RISE AND PROGRESS OF THE ARTS OF DESIGN IN THE UNITED STATES, William Dunlap. Much the richest mine of information on early American painters, sculptors, architects, engravers, miniaturists, etc. The only source of information for scores of artists, the major primary source for many others. Unabridged reprint of rare original 1834 edition, with new introduction by James T. Flexner, and 394 new illustrations. Edited by Rita Weiss. 6⅝ x 9⅝.

21695-0, 21696-9, 21697-7 Three volumes, Paperbound $13.50

EPOCHS OF CHINESE AND JAPANESE ART, Ernest F. Fenollosa. From primitive Chinese art to the 20th century, thorough history, explanation of every important art period and form, including Japanese woodcuts; main stress on China and Japan, but Tibet, Korea also included. Still unexcelled for its detailed, rich coverage of cultural background, aesthetic elements, diffusion studies, particularly of the historical period. 2nd, 1913 edition. 242 illustrations. lii + 439pp. of text.

20364-6, 20365-4 Two volumes, Paperbound $6.00

THE GENTLE ART OF MAKING ENEMIES, James A. M. Whistler. Greatest wit of his day deflates Oscar Wilde, Ruskin, Swinburne; strikes back at inane critics, exhibitions, art journalism; aesthetics of impressionist revolution in most striking form. Highly readable classic by great painter. Reproduction of edition designed by Whistler. Introduction by Alfred Werner. xxxvi + 334pp.

21875-9 Paperbound $2.50

VISUAL ILLUSIONS: THEIR CAUSES, CHARACTERISTICS, AND APPLICATIONS, Matthew Luckiesh. Thorough description and discussion of optical illusion, geometric and perspective, particularly; size and shape distortions, illusions of color, of motion; natural illusions; use of illusion in art and magic, industry, etc. Most useful today with op art, also for classical art. Scores of effects illustrated. Introduction by William H. Ittleson. 100 illustrations. xxi + 252pp.

21530-X Paperbound $2.00

A HANDBOOK OF ANATOMY FOR ART STUDENTS, Arthur Thomson. Thorough, virtually exhaustive coverage of skeletal structure, musculature, etc. Full text, supplemented by anatomical diagrams and drawings and by photographs of undraped figures. Unique in its comparison of male and female forms, pointing out differences of contour, texture, form. 211 figures, 40 drawings, 86 photographs. xx + 459pp. 5⅜ x 8⅜.

21163-0 Paperbound $3.50

150 MASTERPIECES OF DRAWING, Selected by Anthony Toney. Full page reproductions of drawings from the early 16th to the end of the 18th century, all beautifully reproduced: Rembrandt, Michelangelo, Dürer, Fragonard, Urs, Graf, Wouwerman, many others. First-rate browsing book, model book for artists. xviii + 150pp. 8⅜ x 11¼.

21032-4 Paperbound $2.50

THE LATER WORK OF AUBREY BEARDSLEY, Aubrey Beardsley. Exotic, erotic, ironic masterpieces in full maturity: Comedy Ballet, Venus and Tannhauser, Pierrot, Lysistrata, Rape of the Lock, Savoy material, Ali Baba, Volpone, etc. This material revolutionized the art world, and is still powerful, fresh, brilliant. With *The Early Work,* all Beardsley's finest work. 174 plates, 2 in color. xiv + 176pp. 8⅛ x 11.

21817-1 Paperbound $3.00

DRAWINGS OF REMBRANDT, Rembrandt van Rijn. Complete reproduction of fabulously rare edition by Lippmann and Hofstede de Groot, completely reedited, updated, improved by Prof. Seymour Slive, Fogg Museum. Portraits, Biblical sketches, landscapes, Oriental types, nudes, episodes from classical mythology—All Rembrandt's fertile genius. Also selection of drawings by his pupils and followers. "Stunning volumes," *Saturday Review.* 550 illustrations. lxxviii + 552pp. 9⅛ x 12¼.

21485-0, 21486-9 Two volumes, Paperbound $10.00

THE DISASTERS OF WAR, Francisco Goya. One of the masterpieces of Western civilization—83 etchings that record Goya's shattering, bitter reaction to the Napoleonic war that swept through Spain after the insurrection of 1808 and to war in general. Reprint of the first edition, with three additional plates from Boston's Museum of Fine Arts. All plates facsimile size. Introduction by Philip Hofer, Fogg Museum. v + 97pp. 9⅜ x 8¼.

21872-4 Paperbound $2.00

GRAPHIC WORKS OF ODILON REDON. Largest collection of Redon's graphic works ever assembled: 172 lithographs, 28 etchings and engravings, 9 drawings. These include some of his most famous works. All the plates from *Odilon Redon: oeuvre graphique complet,* plus additional plates. New introduction and caption translations by Alfred Werner. 209 illustrations. xxvii + 209pp. 9⅛ x 12¼.

21966-8 Paperbound $4.00

DESIGN BY ACCIDENT; A BOOK OF "ACCIDENTAL EFFECTS" FOR ARTISTS AND DESIGNERS, James F. O'Brien. Create your own unique, striking, imaginative effects by "controlled accident" interaction of materials: paints and lacquers, oil and water based paints, splatter, crackling materials, shatter, similar items. Everything you do will be different; first book on this limitless art, so useful to both fine artist and commercial artist. Full instructions. 192 plates showing "accidents," 8 in color. viii + 215pp. 8⅜ x 11¼.　　　　　　　　　　21942-9 Paperbound $3.50

THE BOOK OF SIGNS, Rudolf Koch. Famed German type designer draws 493 beautiful symbols: religious, mystical, alchemical, imperial, property marks, runes, etc. Remarkable fusion of traditional and modern. Good for suggestions of timelessness, smartness, modernity. Text. vi + 104pp. 6⅛ x 9¼.
20162-7 Paperbound $1.25

HISTORY OF INDIAN AND INDONESIAN ART, Ananda K. Coomaraswamy. An unabridged republication of one of the finest books by a great scholar in Eastern art. Rich in descriptive material, history, social backgrounds; Sunga reliefs, Rajput paintings, Gupta temples, Burmese frescoes, textiles, jewelry, sculpture, etc. 400 photos. viii + 423pp. 6⅜ x 9¾.　　　　　21436-2 Paperbound $4.00

PRIMITIVE ART, Franz Boas. America's foremost anthropologist surveys textiles, ceramics, woodcarving, basketry, metalwork, etc.; patterns, technology, creation of symbols, style origins. All areas of world, but very full on Northwest Coast Indians. More than 350 illustrations of baskets, boxes, totem poles, weapons, etc. 378 pp.
20025-6 Paperbound $3.00

THE GENTLEMAN AND CABINET MAKER'S DIRECTOR, Thomas Chippendale. Full reprint (third edition, 1762) of most influential furniture book of all time, by master cabinetmaker. 200 plates, illustrating chairs, sofas, mirrors, tables, cabinets, plus 24 photographs of surviving pieces. Biographical introduction by N. Bienenstock. vi + 249pp. 9⅞ x 12¾.　　　　　21601-2 Paperbound $4.00

AMERICAN ANTIQUE FURNITURE, Edgar G. Miller, Jr. The basic coverage of all American furniture before 1840. Individual chapters cover type of furniture—clocks, tables, sideboards, etc.—chronologically, with inexhaustible wealth of data. More than 2100 photographs, all identified, commented on. Essential to all early American collectors. Introduction by H. E. Keyes. vi + 1106pp. 7⅞ x 10¾.
21599-7, 21600-4 Two volumes, Paperbound $11.00

PENNSYLVANIA DUTCH AMERICAN FOLK ART, Henry J. Kauffman. 279 photos, 28 drawings of tulipware, Fraktur script, painted tinware, toys, flowered furniture, quilts, samplers, hex signs, house interiors, etc. Full descriptive text. Excellent for tourist, rewarding for designer, collector. Map. 146pp. 7⅞ x 10¾.
21205-X Paperbound $2.50

EARLY NEW ENGLAND GRAVESTONE RUBBINGS, Edmund V. Gillon, Jr. 43 photographs, 226 carefully reproduced rubbings show heavily symbolic, sometimes macabre early gravestones, up to early 19th century. Remarkable early American primitive art, occasionally strikingly beautiful; always powerful. Text. xxvi + 207pp. 8⅜ x 11¼.　　　　　　　　21380-3 Paperbound $3.50

ALPHABETS AND ORNAMENTS, Ernst Lehner. Well-known pictorial source for decorative alphabets, script examples, cartouches, frames, decorative title pages, calligraphic initials, borders, similar material. 14th to 19th century, mostly European. Useful in almost any graphic arts designing, varied styles. 750 illustrations. 256pp. 7 x 10.   21905-4 Paperbound $4.00

PAINTING: A CREATIVE APPROACH, Norman Colquhoun. For the beginner simple guide provides an instructive approach to painting: major stumbling blocks for beginner; overcoming them, technical points; paints and pigments; oil painting; watercolor and other media and color. New section on "plastic" paints. Glossary. Formerly *Paint Your Own Pictures*. 221pp.   22000-1 Paperbound $1.75

THE ENJOYMENT AND USE OF COLOR, Walter Sargent. Explanation of the relations between colors themselves and between colors in nature and art, including hundreds of little-known facts about color values, intensities, effects of high and low illumination, complementary colors. Many practical hints for painters, references to great masters. 7 color plates, 29 illustrations. x + 274pp.
20944-X Paperbound $2.75

THE NOTEBOOKS OF LEONARDO DA VINCI, compiled and edited by Jean Paul Richter. 1566 extracts from original manuscripts reveal the full range of Leonardo's versatile genius: all his writings on painting, sculpture, architecture, anatomy, astronomy, geography, topography, physiology, mining, music, etc., in both Italian and English, with 186 plates of manuscript pages and more than 500 additional drawings. Includes studies for the Last Supper, the lost Sforza monument, and other works. Total of xlvii + 866pp. 7⅞ x 10¾.
22572-0, 22573-9 Two volumes, Paperbound $10.00

MONTGOMERY WARD CATALOGUE OF 1895. Tea gowns, yards of flannel and pillow-case lace, stereoscopes, books of gospel hymns, the New Improved Singer Sewing Machine, side saddles, milk skimmers, straight-edged razors, high-button shoes, spittoons, and on and on . . . listing some 25,000 items, practically all illustrated. Essential to the shoppers of the 1890's, it is our truest record of the spirit of the period. Unaltered reprint of Issue No. 57, Spring and Summer 1895. Introduction by Boris Emmet. Innumerable illustrations. xiii + 624pp. 8½ x 11⅝.
22377-9 Paperbound $6.95

THE CRYSTAL PALACE EXHIBITION ILLUSTRATED CATALOGUE (LONDON, 1851). One of the wonders of the modern world—the Crystal Palace Exhibition in which all the nations of the civilized world exhibited their achievements in the arts and sciences—presented in an equally important illustrated catalogue. More than 1700 items pictured with accompanying text—ceramics, textiles, cast-iron work, carpets, pianos, sleds, razors, wall-papers, billiard tables, beehives, silverware and hundreds of other artifacts—represent the focal point of Victorian culture in the Western World. Probably the largest collection of Victorian decorative art ever assembled— indispensable for antiquarians and designers. Unabridged republication of the Art-Journal Catalogue of the Great Exhibition of 1851, with all terminal essays. New introduction by John Gloag, F.S.A. xxxiv + 426pp. 9 x 12.
22503-8 Paperbound $4.50

A History of Costume, Carl Köhler. Definitive history, based on surviving pieces of clothing primarily, and paintings, statues, etc. secondarily. Highly readable text, supplemented by 594 illustrations of costumes of the ancient Mediterranean peoples, Greece and Rome, the Teutonic prehistoric period; costumes of the Middle Ages, Renaissance, Baroque, 18th and 19th centuries. Clear, measured patterns are provided for many clothing articles. Approach is practical throughout. Enlarged by Emma von Sichart. 464pp. 21030-8 Paperbound $3.50

Oriental Rugs, Antique and Modern, Walter A. Hawley. A complete and authoritative treatise on the Oriental rug—where they are made, by whom and how, designs and symbols, characteristics in detail of the six major groups, how to distinguish them and how to buy them. Detailed technical data is provided on periods, weaves, warps, wefts, textures, sides, ends and knots, although no technical background is required for an understanding. 11 color plates, 80 halftones, 4 maps. vi + 320pp. 6⅛ x 9⅛. 22366-3 Paperbound $5.00

Ten Books on Architecture, Vitruvius. By any standards the most important book on architecture ever written. Early Roman discussion of aesthetics of building, construction methods, orders, sites, and every other aspect of architecture has inspired, instructed architecture for about 2,000 years. Stands behind Palladio, Michelangelo, Bramante, Wren, countless others. Definitive Morris H. Morgan translation. 68 illustrations. xii + 331pp. 20645-9 Paperbound $3.50

The Four Books of Architecture, Andrea Palladio. Translated into every major Western European language in the two centuries following its publication in 1570, this has been one of the most influential books in the history of architecture. Complete reprint of the 1738 Isaac Ware edition. New introduction by Adolf Placzek, Columbia Univ. 216 plates. xxii + 110pp. of text. 9½ x 12¾. 21308-0 Clothbound $10.00

Sticks and Stones: A Study of American Architecture and Civilization, Lewis Mumford.One of the great classics of American cultural history. American architecture from the medieval-inspired earliest forms to the early 20th century; evolution of structure and style, and reciprocal influences on environment. 21 photographic illustrations. 238pp. 20202-X Paperbound $2.00

The American Builder's Companion, Asher Benjamin. The most widely used early 19th century architectural style and source book, for colonial up into Greek Revival periods. Extensive development of geometry of carpentering, construction of sashes, frames, doors, stairs; plans and elevations of domestic and other buildings. Hundreds of thousands of houses were built according to this book, now invaluable to historians, architects, restorers, etc. 1827 edition. 59 plates. 114pp. 7⅞ x 10¾. 22236-5 Paperbound $3.50

Dutch Houses in the Hudson Valley Before 1776, Helen Wilkinson Reynolds. The standard survey of the Dutch colonial house and outbuildings, with constructional features, decoration, and local history associated with individual homesteads. Introduction by Franklin D. Roosevelt. Map. 150 illustrations. 469pp. 6⅝ x 9¼. 21469-9 Paperbound $4.00

THE ARCHITECTURE OF COUNTRY HOUSES, Andrew J. Downing. Together with Vaux's *Villas and Cottages* this is the basic book for Hudson River Gothic architecture of the middle Victorian period. Full, sound discussions of general aspects of housing, architecture, style, decoration, furnishing, together with scores of detailed house plans, illustrations of specific buildings, accompanied by full text. Perhaps the most influential single American architectural book. 1850 edition. Introduction by J. Stewart Johnson. 321 figures, 34 architectural designs. xvi + 560pp.
22003-6 Paperbound $4.00

LOST EXAMPLES OF COLONIAL ARCHITECTURE, John Mead Howells. Full-page photographs of buildings that have disappeared or been so altered as to be denatured, including many designed by major early American architects. 245 plates. xvii + 248pp. 7⅞ x 10¾. 21143-6 Paperbound $3.50

DOMESTIC ARCHITECTURE OF THE AMERICAN COLONIES AND OF THE EARLY REPUBLIC, Fiske Kimball. Foremost architect and restorer of Williamsburg and Monticello covers nearly 200 homes between 1620-1825. Architectural details, construction, style features, special fixtures, floor plans, etc. Generally considered finest work in its area. 219 illustrations of houses, doorways, windows, capital mantels. xx + 314pp. 7⅞ x 10¾. 21743-4 Paperbound $4.00

EARLY AMERICAN ROOMS: 1650-1858, edited by Russell Hawes Kettell. Tour of 12 rooms, each representative of a different era in American history and each furnished, decorated, designed and occupied in the style of the era. 72 plans and elevations, 8-page color section, etc., show fabrics, wall papers, arrangements, etc. Full descriptive text. xvii + 200pp. of text. 8⅜ x 11¼.
21633-0 Paperbound $5.00

THE FITZWILLIAM VIRGINAL BOOK, edited by J. Fuller Maitland and W. B. Squire. Full modern printing of famous early 17th-century ms. volume of 300 works by Morley, Byrd, Bull, Gibbons, etc. For piano or other modern keyboard instrument; easy to read format. xxxvi + 938pp. 8⅜ x 11.
21068-5, 21069-3 Two volumes, Paperbound $10.00

KEYBOARD MUSIC, Johann Sebastian Bach. Bach Gesellschaft edition. A rich selection of Bach's masterpieces for the harpsichord: the six English Suites, six French Suites, the six Partitas (Clavierübung part I), the Goldberg Variations (Clavierübung part IV), the fifteen Two-Part Inventions and the fifteen Three-Part Sinfonias. Clearly reproduced on large sheets with ample margins; eminently playable. vi + 312pp. 8⅛ x 11. 22360-4 Paperbound $5.00

THE MUSIC OF BACH: AN INTRODUCTION, Charles Sanford Terry. A fine, nontechnical introduction to Bach's music, both instrumental and vocal. Covers organ music, chamber music, passion music, other types. Analyzes themes, developments, innovations. x + 114pp. 21075-8 Paperbound $1.25

BEETHOVEN AND HIS NINE SYMPHONIES, Sir George Grove. Noted British musicologist provides best history, analysis, commentary on symphonies. Very thorough, rigorously accurate; necessary to both advanced student and amateur music lover. 436 musical passages. vii + 407 pp. 20334-4 Paperbound $2.75

JOHANN SEBASTIAN BACH, Philipp Spitta. One of the great classics of musicology, this definitive analysis of Bach's music (and life) has never been surpassed. Lucid, nontechnical analyses of hundreds of pieces (30 pages devoted to St. Matthew Passion, 26 to B Minor Mass). Also includes major analysis of 18th-century music. 450 musical examples. 40-page musical supplement. Total of xx + 1799pp.

(EUK) 22278-0, 22279-9 Two volumes, Clothbound $17.50

MOZART AND HIS PIANO CONCERTOS, Cuthbert Girdlestone. The only full-length study of an important area of Mozart's creativity. Provides detailed analyses of all 23 concertos, traces inspirational sources. 417 musical examples. Second edition. 509pp. (USO) 21271-8 Paperbound $3.50

THE PERFECT WAGNERITE: A COMMENTARY ON THE NIBLUNG'S RING, George Bernard Shaw. Brilliant and still relevant criticism in remarkable essays on Wagner's Ring cycle, Shaw's ideas on political and social ideology behind the plots, role of Leitmotifs, vocal requisites, etc. Prefaces. xxi + 136pp.

21707-8 Paperbound $1.50

DON GIOVANNI, W. A. Mozart. Complete libretto, modern English translation; biographies of composer and librettist; accounts of early performances and critical reaction. Lavishly illustrated. All the material you need to understand and appreciate this great work. Dover Opera Guide and Libretto Series; translated and introduced by Ellen Bleiler. 92 illustrations. 209pp.

21134-7 Paperbound $2.00

HIGH FIDELITY SYSTEMS: A LAYMAN'S GUIDE, Roy F. Allison. All the basic information you need for setting up your own audio system: high fidelity and stereo record players, tape records, F.M. Connections, adjusting tone arm, cartridge, checking needle alignment, positioning speakers, phasing speakers, adjusting hums, trouble-shooting, maintenance, and similar topics. Enlarged 1965 edition. More than 50 charts, diagrams, photos. iv + 91pp. 21514-8 Paperbound $1.25

REPRODUCTION OF SOUND, Edgar Villchur. Thorough coverage for laymen of high fidelity systems, reproducing systems in general, needles, amplifiers, preamps, loudspeakers, feedback, explaining physical background. "A rare talent for making technicalities vividly comprehensible," R. Darrell, *High Fidelity*. 69 figures. iv + 92pp. 21515-6 Paperbound $1.25

HEAR ME TALKIN' TO YA: THE STORY OF JAZZ AS TOLD BY THE MEN WHO MADE IT, Nat Shapiro and Nat Hentoff. Louis Armstrong, Fats Waller, Jo Jones, Clarence Williams, Billy Holiday, Duke Ellington, Jelly Roll Morton and dozens of other jazz greats tell how it was in Chicago's South Side, New Orleans, depression Harlem and the modern West Coast as jazz was born and grew. xvi + 429pp.

21726-4 Paperbound $2.50

FABLES OF AESOP, translated by Sir Roger L'Estrange. A reproduction of the very rare 1931 Paris edition; a selection of the most interesting fables, together with 50 imaginative drawings by Alexander Calder. v + 128pp. 6½x9¼.

21780-9 Paperbound $1.50

AGAINST THE GRAIN (A REBOURS), Joris K. Huysmans. Filled with weird images, evidences of a bizarre imagination, exotic experiments with hallucinatory drugs, rich tastes and smells and the diversions of its sybarite hero Duc Jean des Esseintes, this classic novel pushed 19th-century literary decadence to its limits. Full unabridged edition. Do not confuse this with abridged editions generally sold. Introduction by Havelock Ellis. xlix + 206pp. 22190-3 Paperbound $2.00

VARIORUM SHAKESPEARE: HAMLET. Edited by Horace H. Furness; a landmark of American scholarship. Exhaustive footnotes and appendices treat all doubtful words and phrases, as well as suggested critical emendations throughout the play's history. First volume contains editor's own text, collated with all Quartos and Folios. Second volume contains full first Quarto, translations of Shakespeare's sources (Belleforest, and Saxo Grammaticus), Der Bestrafte Brudermord, and many essays on critical and historical points of interest by major authorities of past and present. Includes details of staging and costuming over the years. By far the best edition available for serious students of Shakespeare. Total of xx + 905pp. 21004-9, 21005-7, 2 volumes, Paperbound $7.00

A LIFE OF WILLIAM SHAKESPEARE, Sir Sidney Lee. This is the standard life of Shakespeare, summarizing everything known about Shakespeare and his plays. Incredibly rich in material, broad in coverage, clear and judicious, it has served thousands as the best introduction to Shakespeare. 1931 edition. 9 plates. xxix + 792pp. (USO) 21967-4 Paperbound $3.75

MASTERS OF THE DRAMA, John Gassner. Most comprehensive history of the drama in print, covering every tradition from Greeks to modern Europe and America, including India, Far East, etc. Covers more than 800 dramatists, 2000 plays, with biographical material, plot summaries, theatre history, criticism, etc. "Best of its kind in English," *New Republic*. 77 illustrations. xxii + 890pp. 20100-7 Clothbound $8.50

THE EVOLUTION OF THE ENGLISH LANGUAGE, George McKnight. The growth of English, from the 14th century to the present. Unusual, non-technical account presents basic information in very interesting form: sound shifts, change in grammar and syntax, vocabulary growth, similar topics. Abundantly illustrated with quotations. Formerly *Modern English in the Making*. xii + 590pp. 21932-1 Paperbound $3.50

AN ETYMOLOGICAL DICTIONARY OF MODERN ENGLISH, Ernest Weekley. Fullest, richest work of its sort, by foremost British lexicographer. Detailed word histories, including many colloquial and archaic words; extensive quotations. Do not confuse this with the Concise Etymological Dictionary, which is much abridged. Total of xxvii + 830pp. 6½ x 9¼. 21873-2, 21874-0 Two volumes, Paperbound $6.00

FLATLAND: A ROMANCE OF MANY DIMENSIONS, E. A. Abbott. Classic of science-fiction explores ramifications of life in a two-dimensional world, and what happens when a three-dimensional being intrudes. Amusing reading, but also useful as introduction to thought about hyperspace. Introduction by Banesh Hoffmann. 16 illustrations. xx + 103pp. 20001-9 Paperbound $1.00

POEMS OF ANNE BRADSTREET, edited with an introduction by Robert Hutchinson. A new selection of poems by America's first poet and perhaps the first significant woman poet in the English language. 48 poems display her development in works of considerable variety—love poems, domestic poems, religious meditations, formal elegies, "quaternions," etc. Notes, bibliography. viii + 222pp.

22160-1 Paperbound $2.00

THREE GOTHIC NOVELS: THE CASTLE OF OTRANTO BY HORACE WALPOLE; VATHEK BY WILLIAM BECKFORD; THE VAMPYRE BY JOHN POLIDORI, WITH FRAGMENT OF A NOVEL BY LORD BYRON, edited by E. F. Bleiler. The first Gothic novel, by Walpole; the finest Oriental tale in English, by Beckford; powerful Romantic supernatural story in versions by Polidori and Byron. All extremely important in history of literature; all still exciting, packed with supernatural thrills, ghosts, haunted castles, magic, etc. xl + 291pp.

21232-7 Paperbound $2.50

THE BEST TALES OF HOFFMANN, E. T. A. Hoffmann. 10 of Hoffmann's most important stories, in modern re-editings of standard translations: Nutcracker and the King of Mice, Signor Formica, Automata, The Sandman, Rath Krespel, The Golden Flowerpot, Master Martin the Cooper, The Mines of Falun, The King's Betrothed, A New Year's Eve Adventure. 7 illustrations by Hoffmann. Edited by E. F. Bleiler. xxxix + 419pp. 21793-0 Paperbound $3.00

GHOST AND HORROR STORIES OF AMBROSE BIERCE, Ambrose Bierce. 23 strikingly modern stories of the horrors latent in the human mind: The Eyes of the Panther, The Damned Thing, An Occurrence at Owl Creek Bridge, An Inhabitant of Carcosa, etc., plus the dream-essay, Visions of the Night. Edited by E. F. Bleiler. xxii + 199pp. 20767-6 Paperbound $1.50

BEST GHOST STORIES OF J. S. LeFANU, J. Sheridan LeFanu. Finest stories by Victorian master often considered greatest supernatural writer of all. Carmilla, Green Tea, The Haunted Baronet, The Familiar, and 12 others. Most never before available in the U. S. A. Edited by E. F. Bleiler. 8 illustrations from Victorian publications. xvii + 467pp. 20415-4 Paperbound $3.00

MATHEMATICAL FOUNDATIONS OF INFORMATION THEORY, A. I. Khinchin. Comprehensive introduction to work of Shannon, McMillan, Feinstein and Khinchin, placing these investigations on a rigorous mathematical basis. Covers entropy concept in probability theory, uniqueness theorem, Shannon's inequality, ergodic sources, the E property, martingale concept, noise, Feinstein's fundamental lemma, Shanon's first and second theorems. Translated by R. A. Silverman and M. D. Friedman. iii + 120pp. 60434-9 Paperbound $1.75

SEVEN SCIENCE FICTION NOVELS, H. G. Wells. The standard collection of the great novels. Complete, unabridged. *First Men in the Moon, Island of Dr. Moreau, War of the Worlds, Food of the Gods, Invisible Man, Time Machine, In the Days of the Comet.* Not only science fiction fans, but every educated person owes it to himself to read these novels. 1015pp. 20264-X Clothbound $5.00

LAST AND FIRST MEN AND STAR MAKER, TWO SCIENCE FICTION NOVELS, Olaf Stapledon. Greatest future histories in science fiction. In the first, human intelligence is the "hero," through strange paths of evolution, interplanetary invasions, incredible technologies, near extinctions and reemergences. Star Maker describes the quest of a band of star rovers for intelligence itself, through time and space: weird inhuman civilizations, crustacean minds, symbiotic worlds, etc. Complete, unabridged. v + 438pp. 21962-3 Paperbound $2.50

THREE PROPHETIC NOVELS, H. G. WELLS. Stages of a consistently planned future for mankind. *When the Sleeper Wakes,* and *A Story of the Days to Come,* anticipate *Brave New World* and *1984,* in the 21st Century; *The Time Machine,* only complete version in print, shows farther future and the end of mankind. All show Wells's greatest gifts as storyteller and novelist. Edited by E. F. Bleiler. x + 335pp. (USO) 20605-X Paperbound $2.50

THE DEVIL'S DICTIONARY, Ambrose Bierce. America's own Oscar Wilde—Ambrose Bierce—offers his barbed iconoclastic wisdom in over 1,000 definitions hailed by H. L. Mencken as "some of the most gorgeous witticisms in the English language." 145pp. 20487-1 Paperbound $1.25

MAX AND MORITZ, Wilhelm Busch. Great children's classic, father of comic strip, of two bad boys, Max and Moritz. Also Ker and Plunk (Plisch und Plumm), Cat and Mouse, Deceitful Henry, Ice-Peter, The Boy and the Pipe, and five other pieces. Original German, with English translation. Edited by H. Arthur Klein; translations by various hands and H. Arthur Klein. vi + 216pp.
20181-3 Paperbound $2.00

PIGS IS PIGS AND OTHER FAVORITES, Ellis Parker Butler. The title story is one of the best humor short stories, as Mike Flannery obfuscates biology and English. Also included, That Pup of Murchison's, The Great American Pie Company, and Perkins of Portland. 14 illustrations. v + 109pp. 21532-6 Paperbound $1.25

THE PETERKIN PAPERS, Lucretia P. Hale. It takes genius to be as stupidly mad as the Peterkins, as they decide to become wise, celebrate the "Fourth," keep a cow, and otherwise strain the resources of the Lady from Philadelphia. Basic book of American humor. 153 illustrations. 219pp. 20794-3 Paperbound $1.50

PERRAULT'S FAIRY TALES, translated by A. E. Johnson and S. R. Littlewood, with 34 full-page illustrations by Gustave Doré. All the original Perrault stories—Cinderella, Sleeping Beauty, Bluebeard, Little Red Riding Hood, Puss in Boots, Tom Thumb, etc.—with their witty verse morals and the magnificent illustrations of Doré. One of the five or six great books of European fairy tales. viii + 117pp. 8⅛ x 11. 22311-6 Paperbound $2.00

OLD HUNGARIAN FAIRY TALES, Baroness Orczy. Favorites translated and adapted by author of the *Scarlet Pimpernel.* Eight fairy tales include "The Suitors of Princess Fire-Fly," "The Twin Hunchbacks," "Mr. Cuttlefish's Love Story," and "The Enchanted Cat." This little volume of magic and adventure will captivate children as it has for generations. 90 drawings by Montagu Barstow. 96pp.
(USO) 22293-4 Paperbound $1.95

THE RED FAIRY BOOK, Andrew Lang. Lang's color fairy books have long been children's favorites. This volume includes Rapunzel, Jack and the Bean-stalk and 35 other stories, familiar and unfamiliar. 4 plates, 93 illustrations x + 367pp.
21673-X Paperbound $2.50

THE BLUE FAIRY BOOK, Andrew Lang. Lang's tales come from all countries and all times. Here are 37 tales from Grimm, the Arabian Nights, Greek Mythology, and other fascinating sources. 8 plates, 130 illustrations. xi + 390pp.
21437-0 Paperbound $2.50

HOUSEHOLD STORIES BY THE BROTHERS GRIMM. Classic English-language edition of the well-known tales — Rumpelstiltskin, Snow White, Hansel and Gretel, The Twelve Brothers, Faithful John, Rapunzel, Tom Thumb (52 stories in all). Translated into simple, straightforward English by Lucy Crane. Ornamented with head-pieces, vignettes, elaborate decorative initials and a dozen full-page illustrations by Walter Crane. x + 269pp.
21080-4 Paperbound $2.50

THE MERRY ADVENTURES OF ROBIN HOOD, Howard Pyle. The finest modern versions of the traditional ballads and tales about the great English outlaw. Howard Pyle's complete prose version, with every word, every illustration of the first edition. Do not confuse this facsimile of the original (1883) with modern editions that change text or illustrations. 23 plates plus many page decorations. xxii + 296pp.
22043-5 Paperbound $2.50

THE STORY OF KING ARTHUR AND HIS KNIGHTS, Howard Pyle. The finest children's version of the life of King Arthur; brilliantly retold by Pyle, with 48 of his most imaginative illustrations. xviii + 313pp. 6⅛ x 9¼.
21445-1 Paperbound $2.50

THE WONDERFUL WIZARD OF OZ, L. Frank Baum. America's finest children's book in facsimile of first edition with all Denslow illustrations in full color. The edition a child should have. Introduction by Martin Gardner. 23 color plates, scores of drawings. iv + 267pp.
20691-2 Paperbound $2.50

THE MARVELOUS LAND OF OZ, L. Frank Baum. The second Oz book, every bit as imaginative as the Wizard. The hero is a boy named Tip, but the Scarecrow and the Tin Woodman are back, as is the Oz magic. 16 color plates, 120 drawings by John R. Neill. 287pp.
20692-0 Paperbound $2.50

THE MAGICAL MONARCH OF MO, L. Frank Baum. Remarkable adventures in a land even stranger than Oz. The best of Baum's books not in the Oz series. 15 color plates and dozens of drawings by Frank Verbeck. xviii + 237pp.
21892-9 Paperbound $2.25

THE BAD CHILD'S BOOK OF BEASTS, MORE BEASTS FOR WORSE CHILDREN, A MORAL ALPHABET, Hilaire Belloc. Three complete humor classics in one volume. Be kind to the frog, and do not call him names . . . and 28 other whimsical animals. Familiar favorites and some not so well known. Illustrated by Basil Blackwell. 156pp.
(USO) 20749-8 Paperbound $1.50

EAST O' THE SUN AND WEST O' THE MOON, George W. Dasent. Considered the best of all translations of these Norwegian folk tales, this collection has been enjoyed by generations of children (and folklorists too). Includes True and Untrue, Why the Sea is Salt, East O' the Sun and West O' the Moon, Why the Bear is Stumpy-Tailed, Boots and the Troll, The Cock and the Hen, Rich Peter the Pedlar, and 52 more. The only edition with all 59 tales. 77 illustrations by Erik Werenskiold and Theodor Kittelsen. xv + 418pp. 22521-6 Paperbound $3.50

GOOPS AND HOW TO BE THEM, Gelett Burgess. Classic of tongue-in-cheek humor, masquerading as etiquette book. 87 verses, twice as many cartoons, show mischievous Goops as they demonstrate to children virtues of table manners, neatness, courtesy, etc. Favorite for generations. viii + 88pp. 6½ x 9¼. 22233-0 Paperbound $1.25

ALICE'S ADVENTURES UNDER GROUND, Lewis Carroll. The first version, quite different from the final *Alice in Wonderland,* printed out by Carroll himself with his own illustrations. Complete facsimile of the "million dollar" manuscript Carroll gave to Alice Liddell in 1864. Introduction by Martin Gardner. viii + 96pp. Title and dedication pages in color. 21482-6 Paperbound $1.25

THE BROWNIES, THEIR BOOK, Palmer Cox. Small as mice, cunning as foxes, exuberant and full of mischief, the Brownies go to the zoo, toy shop, seashore, circus, etc., in 24 verse adventures and 266 illustrations. Long a favorite, since their first appearance in St. Nicholas Magazine. xi + 144pp. 6⅝ x 9¼. 21265-3 Paperbound $1.75

SONGS OF CHILDHOOD, Walter De La Mare. Published (under the pseudonym Walter Ramal) when De La Mare was only 29, this charming collection has long been a favorite children's book. A facsimile of the first edition in paper, the 47 poems capture the simplicity of the nursery rhyme and the ballad, including such lyrics as I Met Eve, Tartary, The Silver Penny. vii + 106pp. 21972-0 Paperbound $1.25

THE COMPLETE NONSENSE OF EDWARD LEAR, Edward Lear. The finest 19th-century humorist-cartoonist in full: all nonsense limericks, zany alphabets, Owl and Pussycat, songs, nonsense botany, and more than 500 illustrations by Lear himself. Edited by Holbrook Jackson. xxix + 287pp. (USO) 20167-8 Paperbound $2.00

BILLY WHISKERS: THE AUTOBIOGRAPHY OF A GOAT, Frances Trego Montgomery. A favorite of children since the early 20th century, here are the escapades of that rambunctious, irresistible and mischievous goat—Billy Whiskers. Much in the spirit of *Peck's Bad Boy,* this is a book that children never tire of reading or hearing. All the original familiar illustrations by W. H. Fry are included: 6 color plates, 18 black and white drawings. 159pp. 22345-0 Paperbound $2.00

MOTHER GOOSE MELODIES. Faithful republication of the fabulously rare Munroe and Francis "copyright 1833" Boston edition—the most important Mother Goose collection, usually referred to as the "original." Familiar rhymes plus many rare ones, with wonderful old woodcut illustrations. Edited by E. F. Bleiler. 128pp. 4½ x 6⅜. 22577-1 Paperbound $1.25

Two Little Savages; Being the Adventures of Two Boys Who Lived as Indians and What They Learned, Ernest Thompson Seton. Great classic of nature and boyhood provides a vast range of woodlore in most palatable form, a genuinely entertaining story. Two farm boys build a teepee in woods and live in it for a month, working out Indian solutions to living problems, star lore, birds and animals, plants, etc. 293 illustrations. vii + 286pp.

20985-7 Paperbound $2.50

Peter Piper's Practical Principles of Plain & Perfect Pronunciation. Alliterative jingles and tongue-twisters of surprising charm, that made their first appearance in America about 1830. Republished in full with the spirited woodcut illustrations from this earliest American edition. 32pp. 4½ x 6⅜.

22560-7 Paperbound $1.00

Science Experiments and Amusements for Children, Charles Vivian. 73 easy experiments, requiring only materials found at home or easily available, such as candles, coins, steel wool, etc.; illustrate basic phenomena like vacuum, simple chemical reaction, etc. All safe. Modern, well-planned. Formerly *Science Games for Children.* 102 photos, numerous drawings. 96pp. 6⅛ x 9¼.

21856-2 Paperbound $1.25

An Introduction to Chess Moves and Tactics Simply Explained, Leonard Barden. Informal intermediate introduction, quite strong in explaining reasons for moves. Covers basic material, tactics, important openings, traps, positional play in middle game, end game. Attempts to isolate patterns and recurrent configurations. Formerly *Chess.* 58 figures. 102pp. (USO) 21210-6 Paperbound $1.25

Lasker's Manual of Chess, Dr. Emanuel Lasker. Lasker was not only one of the five great World Champions, he was also one of the ablest expositors, theorists, and analysts. In many ways, his Manual, permeated with his philosophy of battle, filled with keen insights, is one of the greatest works ever written on chess. Filled with analyzed games by the great players. A single-volume library that will profit almost any chess player, beginner or master. 308 diagrams. xli x 349pp.

20640-8 Paperbound $2.75

The Master Book of Mathematical Recreations, Fred Schuh. In opinion of many the finest work ever prepared on mathematical puzzles, stunts, recreations; exhaustively thorough explanations of mathematics involved, analysis of effects, citation of puzzles and games. Mathematics involved is elementary. Translated by F. Göbel. 194 figures. xxiv + 430pp.

22134-2 Paperbound $3.00

Mathematics, Magic and Mystery, Martin Gardner. Puzzle editor for Scientific American explains mathematics behind various mystifying tricks: card tricks, stage "mind reading," coin and match tricks, counting out games, geometric dissections, etc. Probability sets, theory of numbers clearly explained. Also provides more than 400 tricks, guaranteed to work, that you can do. 135 illustrations. xii + 176pp.

20338-2 Paperbound $1.50

MATHEMATICAL PUZZLES FOR BEGINNERS AND ENTHUSIASTS, Geoffrey Mott-Smith. 189 puzzles from easy to difficult—involving arithmetic, logic, algebra, properties of digits, probability, etc.—for enjoyment and mental stimulus. Explanation of mathematical principles behind the puzzles. 135 illustrations. viii + 248pp.
20198-8 Paperbound $1.75

PAPER FOLDING FOR BEGINNERS, William D. Murray and Francis J. Rigney. Easiest book on the market, clearest instructions on making interesting, beautiful origami Sail boats, cups, roosters, frogs that move legs, bonbon boxes, standing birds, etc. 40 projects; more than 275 diagrams and photographs. 94pp.
20713-7 Paperbound $1.00

TRICKS AND GAMES ON THE POOL TABLE, Fred Herrmann. 79 tricks and games— some solitaires, some for two or more players, some competitive games—to entertain you between formal games. Mystifying shots and throws, unusual caroms, tricks involving such props as cork, coins, a hat, etc. Formerly *Fun on the Pool Table*. 77 figures. 95pp.
21814-7 Paperbound $1.00

HAND SHADOWS TO BE THROWN UPON THE WALL: A SERIES OF NOVEL AND AMUSING FIGURES FORMED BY THE HAND, Henry Bursill. Delightful picturebook from great-grandfather's day shows how to make 18 different hand shadows: a bird that flies, duck that quacks, dog that wags his tail, camel, goose, deer, boy, turtle, etc. Only book of its sort. vi + 33pp. 6½ x 9¼. 21779-5 Paperbound $1.00

WHITTLING AND WOODCARVING, E. J. Tangerman. 18th printing of best book on market. "If you can cut a potato you can carve" toys and puzzles, chains, chessmen, caricatures, masks, frames, woodcut blocks, surface patterns, much more. Information on tools, woods, techniques. Also goes into serious wood sculpture from Middle Ages to present, East and West. 464 photos, figures. x + 293pp.
20965-2 Paperbound $2.00

HISTORY OF PHILOSOPHY, Julián Marias. Possibly the clearest, most easily followed, best planned, most useful one-volume history of philosophy on the market; neither skimpy nor overfull. Full details on system of every major philosopher and dozens of less important thinkers from pre-Socratics up to Existentialism and later. Strong on many European figures usually omitted. Has gone through dozens of editions in Europe. 1966 edition, translated by Stanley Appelbaum and Clarence Strowbridge. xviii + 505pp.
21739-6 Paperbound $3.00

YOGA: A SCIENTIFIC EVALUATION, Kovoor T. Behanan. Scientific but non-technical study of physiological results of yoga exercises; done under auspices of Yale U. Relations to Indian thought, to psychoanalysis, etc. 16 photos. xxiii + 270pp.
20505-3 Paperbound $2.50

Prices subject to change without notice.
Available at your book dealer or write for free catalogue to Dept. GI, Dover Publications, Inc., 180 Varick St., N. Y., N. Y. 10014. Dover publishes more than 150 books each year on science, elementary and advanced mathematics, biology, music, art, literary history, social sciences and other areas.